SCIENFITIC ERRORS IN THE QURAN

DR. MAXWELL SHIMBA

Shimba Publishing LLC

Printed in the United States of America

First Printing Edition 2024

Table of Contents

About Quran

Muslims often disarm those who criticize the Qur'an by asking if they had read the Qur'an in Arabic. Whenever we debate with Muslims about the deficiencies, contradictions, absurdities or the violent verses of the Qur'an, their favorite line of defense is *"Can you read Arabic?"* The inference is that all the difficulties of the Qur'an will somehow disappear if we read it in the Arabic language. The Muslim game is that the Qur'an can only be fully understood in Arabic. Therefore, one cannot criticize Islam without knowing Arabic.

Muslims claim that the language of the Qur'an is so unique that an accurate translation of it into another language is virtually impossible. This is a deception by Muslims. They try to silence any criticism that is raised against the Qur'an by resorting to this deception. Since most of us do not understand or speak the original language of the Qur'an, they quickly dismiss our arguments as baseless. We are told that since we do not know Arabic, we are not in a position to raise any objection against the Qur'an. *"Can you read Arabic?"* has often been the battle cry of Muslims when they engage in debates with Christians. Critics of the Qur'an are often reduced to an awkward silence with this Muslim tactic. This lie needs to be exposed.

Firstly, the Qur'an claims to be a universal message for all humanity for all times. If the message is universal, then it must be understood by all people. If the great majority of mankind cannot understand the message, then by definition it is not universal. To claim that we need to know Arabic to understand the Qur'an belies the claim that the Qur'an is a universal message for all humanity. Therefore, this shameful tactic of Muslims comes at a heavy price for them, since Islam cannot be protected in this way without sacrificing its claim to being a universal religion.

Secondly, how many Muslims are able to read the Qur'an in Arabic, let alone with understanding? The great majority of Muslims are not Arabs or Arabic speaking peoples. In fact, the largest Muslim nation, Indonesia, and the second largest Muslim nation, Pakistan, are non-Arabic speaking nations. And to these we can add Iran, Turkey, Malaysia, India (which has a sizeable Muslim population) and many others. In other words, the majority of Muslims have to rely on translations of the Qur'an in their native language in order to understand it. In fact, most Muslims who raise the language objection are non-Arabs who do not understand Arabic. How then did they become Muslims without understanding Arabic?

Additionally, it must be made clear which Arabic is being discussed here. The Arabic of the Qur'an is classical Arabic. Classical Arabic of the Qur'an is totally different from the Arabic of today. In other words, the great majority of modern Arab cannot effectively read the original Arabic Qur'an and understand its meaning. Thus, even Arab Muslims have to rely on translations to understand the Qur'an. It is estimated that fewer than a thousand scholars who read classical Arabic can compose a paragraph in classical Arabic script on a given subject.

Now, what about the billion-plus Muslims who do not even understand modern Arabic? If it is necessary to have a knowledge of classical Arabic to understand the Qur'an correctly, then how can all those non-Arabic speaking Muslims understand the Qur'an? Since it is alleged that it impossible for them to understand the Qur'an correctly in their native language, how then did they become Muslims?

Arabic is a Semitic language related to Hebrew and Aramaic. If these two Biblical languages can be translated into other languages, why not the Arabic of the Qur'an? Why would Muslims want us to believe that the Qur'an alone could not be understood in other languages? Is not Arab a human language?

THE MUSLIM DILEMMA

Muslims fail to realize that there is a serious theological problem with their argument that the Qur'an cannot be translated or fully understood in a language other than Arabic. Consider now the following Qur'anic verses:

Surah 26:192-197: And lo! It is a revelation of the Lord of the Worlds, Which the True Spirit hath brought down upon thy heart, that thou mayest be one of the warners, In plain Arabic speech. And lo, it is in the Scriptures of the men of old. Is it not a token for them that the doctors of the Children of Israel know it? (Pickthall)
Truly it is revelation sent down by the Lord of all the Worlds. The Faithful Ruh brought it down to your heart so you would be one of the Warners in a clear Arabic tongue. It is certainly in the Scriptures of the previous peoples. Is it not indeed a Sign for them that the scholars of the tribe of Israel have knowledge of it? (A. Bewley)

"It is certainly in the Scriptures of the previous peoples." The Scriptures of the previous peoples are the Torah and the Gospel. And these Scriptures were revealed in the Hebrew and Greek languages with a small portion of it in Aramaic. After saying that the Qur'an was revealed in *"plain Arabic speech,"* the above Qur'anic verses continue on to state that the Qur'an is *"in the Scriptures of the previous peoples."* How can the contents of the Qur'an which are written in *"plain Arabic speech"* be written in the previous Scriptures when the previous Scriptures were not revealed in the Arabic language?

Of course, for the Qur'an to be written in the previous Scriptures, it must be written in the languages of the previous Scriptures. Since the Bible was revealed centuries before the Qur'an, this presupposes that the Qur'an which was written in *"plain Arabic speech"* was transmitted accurately in the languages of the Bible before the arrival of the Qur'an. This demonstrates that the Qur'an can be accurately translated into other languages. And vice versa.

To accept Surah 26:192-197 as divinely inspired, Muslims have to accept as true what these Qur'anic verses actually teach. They have to accept the fact that the Qur'an itself confirms that the Qur'an can be translated into other languages such as Hebrew, Aramaic and Greek. Notice what the Qur'an clearly states: *"Is it not indeed a Sign for them that the scholars of the tribe of Israel have knowledge of it?"* Yes! It can be understood by those who speak a different language such as Hebrew. Additionally, it is important to remember that Greek is not a Semitic language. This fact alone proves that the Arabic of the Qur'an can be translated into languages that have no common roots with it.

Muslims have an option. To believe that the Qur'an which was revealed *"in plain Arabic speech"* is in the *"Scriptures of the previous peoples,"* Muslims have to accept as true that the Qur'an has already been transmitted accurately in the languages of the Bible. This means that the Qur'an can be translated accurately from Arabic into other languages. Alternately, Muslims can choose to believe that the Qur'an cannot be translated accurately into other languages. This would then that they have to believe that the above Qur'anic verses are false. Muslims have to now choose between these two options.

Therefore, the only option left for Muslims come to terms with Allah's revelation in Surah 26:192-197 is to accept the fact that long before the messages of the Qur'an were written in *"plain Arabic,"* these very same messages were written earlier in the Bible in Hebrew, Aramaic and Greek. Should Muslims choose to disagree with this conclusion, it would then mean that the Qur'an is a lie.

The fact that the messages of the Qur'an could be written in Hebrew, Aramaic and Greek proves that the Arabic Qur'an can be translated into Hebrew, Aramaic and Greek and vice-versa. And since the Bible which is written in Hebrew, Aramaic and Greek has been translated accurately into hundreds of languages, it proves that the same can be accomplished with the Qur'an. Thus, there is no validity in the Muslim argument that the Qur'an can only be understood in the Arabic language.

Of course, Christians do not believe that the messages of Qur'an can be found in the Bible. Christians do not believe that the Qur'an is the inspired Word of God. We are only using the above argument to prove that even according to their Qur'an, the Muslim claim is false. The Qur'an itself proves that it can be written and understood in languages other than Arabic.
"CAN YOU READ ARABIC"

The reason for Muslims to come up with the excuse that one should know Arabic to understand the Qur'an is really quite simple. For one, it is the easiest way to silence the critics. However, there is also another reason. Many of those who have read the Qur'an in the language they could understand became shocked by its contents. Their study of Islam's holiest book only reinforced a negative opinion of it. To overcome this dilemma, Muslims scholars came up with a contingency plan to respond to these ones who now question the unethical teachings of the Qur'an. These scholars began to dishonestly claim that an accurate knowledge of the Qur'an can only be accomplished with the understanding of the Arabic language.

This deceit is also conveniently used to silence any critics of the Qur'an. This is a carefully planned deception on the part by Muslims leaders. Is Arabic truly an untranslatable language? The existence of translations of many early Arabic literatures in other languages easily exposes this deceit by Muslims. A classic example of this are the Hadiths. If it is possible to translate the other earlier Arabic works into foreign languages, why cannot the same be done with the Qur'an? If Arabic is truly a barrier for non-Arabs to understand Islam, why did Allah choose this untranslatable language to reveal the Qur'an?

This linguistic objection is only a recent development in Islam. Quite tellingly this development began with the contemporary rejection of Islamic practices by the non-Muslim world. It began when Islam's debased practices such as slavery, the inferior status of women, wife-beating, holy war, religious discrimination, became exposed to the non-Muslim world. Especially today, this linguistic objection has become a much needed defense mechanism for Muslims because of the easy exposé of Islam through the information superhighway – the internet. No other religion makes this absurd claim that the knowledge of a particular language is imperative to the understanding of that religion.

Obviously, the real reason for this illogical linguistic argument is that the information age is now making it possible for the teachings of the Islamic religion to be available to a broader audience. And the contents are highly embarrassing to both Muslim scholars and their faithful flock. Pretending that different meanings exist in Arabic became a means of gaining self-confidence and saving face with others.

The next time when you find a Muslim arguing against any Christian doctrine, just ask him if he can read Hebrew, Aramaic or Koine Greek. If he does not know these languages how can he then form an opinion about something he has read from a translation? If Muslims have the privilege to form an opinion based on a translation of the Holy Bible, why are we not given the same privilege? Why can we not in the same way read and understand the Qur'an? This shows that we do not need to know Arabic to refute the teachings of the Qur'an. Yet Muslims are quite happy to criticize the Bible and Christianity without knowing a single word of Hebrew, Aramaic or Greek.

Muslims do not understand that their flawed logic to defend Islam's absurdities goes against them. If it is possible for Muslims around the world to preach Islam in languages other than Arabic and make converts, why do they then argue that the Qur'an can only be understood in Arabic? How can these new converts to Islam become Muslims without understanding Arabic? In other words, how can new converts to Islam become Muslims without understanding the Qur'an? The language argument is a Muslim tactic to defend the idiocy of Islam. If Islam is indeed the true religion, language will not be a barrier for any sincere honest-hearted persons to discover the truth in it. It must be pointed out that the majority of the translations of the Qur'an are done by devout Muslims. Hence, Muslims cannot claim that there has been deliberate tampering of the text by infidel translators.

Moreover, many of the doctrines of the Qur'an are repeated word for word and explained in the Hadiths. If it is possible for these doctrines, which are recorded in Arabic in the Hadiths, to be translated and understood by the non-Arabic Muslim population, why is it impossible to do the same with the Qur'an? Why is that out of all the books in the world, the Qur'an is the only one that cannot be translated and understood accurately in another language? How is that the Arabic Qur'an is the only one with words and phrases that are literally untranslatable? Does it not sound suspicious? If the language argument is really true, then we must ask the Muslims, "Why in the world would Allah choose to communicate his final revelation for all people in the only language that cannot be understood by all people?" Not even by the majority of the Muslims.

In the first place, it is basically impossible for anyone to learn a new language if they cannot relate it to the wordings of the language they already do know. In other words, if someone wants to learn Arabic, he or she must be able to perceive the meaning of the Arabic words in their own language. They need to mentally translate the Arabic that they are learning into their mother tongue. If this is possible, then it proves that Arabic is not a language that cannot be translated. Therefore, Muslim apologists who insist that one must learn Arabic to understand the Qur'an are committing a logical fallacy. Either the Arabic of the Qur'an is translatable for one to learn it, in which case it would not be necessary to learn Arabic, since one can now rely on the translation. Or it is not translatable, in which case it can never be learned by the non-Arabic speaker.

In order for the Qur'an to be the divine Word of God, every single word in it must be translatable into any language of the world. The Word of God must be clear and understandable for all mankind. Therefore, to claim that the Qur'an is not translatable means it is not the Word of God. It is fraudulent.

THE MOST WIDELY DISTRIBUTED BOOK IN THE WORLD
"The Bible is the most widely read book in history…More copies have been distributed of the Bible than of any other book. The Bible has also been translated more times, and into more languages, than any other book."—"The World Book Encyclopedia."

The true Revelation of God can be conveyed in any language.
Revelation 14:6-7: And I saw another angel flying in midheaven, and he had everlasting good news to declare as glad tidings to those who dwell on the earth, and to every nation and tribe and tongue and people, saying in a loud voice: "Fear God and give him glory."

The Bible is the most widely translated book in history. The complete Bible or portions of it have been translated into more than 2,600 languages and dialects. Over 90 percent of the human family has access to at least part of the Bible in their own language.

Isaiah 11:9: "They will not do any harm or cause any ruin in all my holy mountain; because the earth will certainly be filled with the knowledge of Jehovah as the waters are covering the very sea."

The Bible is well understood because it is published and made available in the various tongues of the people. The Holy Bible, inspired by none other than the Creator of the human languages, has crossed national boundaries and transcended racial and ethnic barriers. Thus, Christians of all nationalities and races can easily understand the message of their Creator. Their clear understanding of the Bible – in their own language – presents the faithful Christians with a unique opportunity to cultivate a close relationship with their heavenly Father. This helps them to develop a significant amount of appreciation for Him – without having to devote their time learning another language that is alien to them. It is well known and it can be confirmed by linguists that learning in one's own mother tongue is better understood than in a second-language. It also has many other advantages.

The God of the Holy Bible understands this. Thus, he has never insisted on making one language more significant than the other. The conveying of the life-saving message of the Bible is the primary concern of our Creator and not the learning of a particular language. That is why the Message of the Holy Bible is truly universal. Even an Arab can obtain the Holy Bible and read it in his mother tongue.

Islam on the other hand requires all Muslims to know Arabic to understand the Qur'an. In fact, Islam requires all Muslims to pray in the Arabic language. No matter in which country a Muslim lives, the mosques will blare out prayers only in Arabic. Does not Allah understand other languages? This bias towards one language somehow elevates those whose mother tongue is Arabic above the non-Arabic Muslim population. And, of course, it is an insult to all other languages. Because of this bias towards one language, most Muslims have to memorize prayers in the Arabic language which most of them do not even understand. More than 80% of Muslims have to pray in a language which is alien to them. Thus, most Muslims have no clue of what they keep repeating, five times a day.

If you find this unbelievable, test this out by asking Muslims. And you will soon find out how many really understand what they are saying to Allah. If they are cannot even converse in Arabic, how can they really understand the Qur'an? It is similar to an American parroting a prayer in romanized Sanskrit. Such is the illogical situation that Muslims find themselves in because of the teachings of Islam. Now, contrast Allah with Jehovah. No matter in which language we speak to our heavenly Father, he listens to us. This is the hallmark of a true Creator:

Psalms 65:2: "O Hearer of prayer, even to you people of all flesh will come."

Isaiah 45:22-24: "Turn to me and be saved, all you who dwell at the ends of the earth; for I am God, and there is no one else. By my own self I have sworn, my mouth has uttered in righteousness a word that will not be revoked: Before me every knee will bend down, and every tongue will confess allegiance to me, saying, 'Surely in Jehovah there are full righteousness and strength."

Romans 10:11-13: For the Scripture says: "None that rests his faith on him will be disappointed." For there is no distinction between Jew and Greek, for there is the same Lord over all, who is rich to all those calling upon him. For "everyone who calls on the name of Jehovah will be saved."

The Holy Bible reveals the Mind of God, the State of Man, the Way of Salvation, the Destiny of Sinners, and the Joy of Believers. Its Doctrines are Holy, its Precepts are Binding, its Decisions are Immutable, its Histories are True, and its Teachings are Divine. And it makes no excuses.

CHAPTER 1

Can "Modern Science" Be Found in the Quran?

From time to time, a specific argument surfaces in discussions across newsgroups, social media, and other platforms. The argument suggests that modern science is embedded within the Qur'an, claiming that the sacred text references various scientific fields, such as astronomy, embryology, geology, and even comets. It is then argued that, because Muhammad could not have known these scientific facts, the Qur'an must be divine.

Rebuttals to this claim typically focus on disputing the scientific points made, with scholars like Andrew Vargo contributing notable work on debunking such assertions (e.g., on the Answering Islam site). While it is relatively straightforward to counter these claims, the repeated task can become tiresome. In this short document, I seek to address not just the individual scientific claims, but the underlying idea of "modern science" in the Qur'an. I contend that the very concept is flawed, and I aim to highlight logical weaknesses in the argument itself. The following points can be used whether the discussion revolves around embryology, geology, or any other scientific subject claimed to be present in the Qur'an.

The paper emerged from a debate on the soc.religion.islam newsgroup about the relationship between rivers and oceans, which explains the references to that topic within this document.

Here are six fundamental flaws in the "modern science proves the Qur'an" argument:

1. **Lack of Alternative Interpretations:** Proponents of the argument fail to allow for other possible interpretations of the Qur'an's verses.
2. **Weakening of Allah's Power:** The argument inadvertently portrays Allah as lacking the power to transcend human understanding.
3. **A Modern Polemic:** The argument is shaped by modern biases and needs, rather than an interpretation of the Qur'an's original message.
4. **Misuse of Science to Judge the Qur'an:** Instead of finding science within the Qur'an, the argument uses modern science to evaluate the Qur'an.
5. **Selective Interpretation:** The method of selective interpretation allows the proof of any claim, regardless of its truth.
6. **Undermining the Qur'an's Authority:** If science is used as the measure to validate the Qur'an, its inherent authority as a divine text is compromised.

Conclusion:

I trust these points will provide helpful insights. What I found particularly enlightening and encouraging were some of the responses from Muslims, several of whom agreed with my perspective and rejected the argument that attempts to use science to promote the Qur'an. For instance, a Muslim named Ibn Abdulrahman noted in reference to point 4 that "this is, in fact, the reason why our scholars generally reject the efforts to proclaim 'science in the Qur'an'" and concluded his response with the phrase "Basically, *Andy is right.*"

1) Those Who Pursue the Argument Leave No Room for Alternative Interpretations

The Qur'an, by its nature, allows for a range of interpretations, and Muslims often hold different views on the meaning of specific verses. This is perfectly valid; exegesis can be challenging, especially when the exact historical context of a verse is unknown. For example, consider the figure of Dhu Al-Qarnayn (or Zul-Qarnain) in the Qur'an. Muslims are divided over his identity, with some (e.g., Yusuf Ali) believing him to be Alexander the Great, while others propose figures like Cyrus the Great. This diversity of interpretation reflects the complexity of understanding the text, and there is ample space for healthy debate.

However, proponents of the argument that "modern science proves the Qur'an" do not rely on the text itself, but rather on their own interpretation of it. In fact, it would be more accurate to label this position as "the belief that an interpretation of the Qur'an that aligns with modern science demonstrates its divine origin." No verse in the Qur'an has been shown to explicitly contain modern scientific facts (see point 2 for further discussion).

Consider, for example, Sura 25:53, which sparked a discussion in the soc.religion.islam newsgroup:

"It is He Who has let free the two bodies of flowing water: One palatable and sweet, and the other salt and bitter; yet has He made a barrier between them, a partition that is forbidden to be passed." (Sura 25:53, Yusuf Ali)

In the debate, a Muslim participant argued that this verse refers to the meeting of large rivers and oceans, where the river can flow into the sea for miles without the two waters mixing. He claimed this phenomenon, recognized by modern science, was described by the Qur'an. He also suggested that the difference in salinity between the waters could be explained by the varying specific gravities of fresh and saltwater.

However, when examining different English translations of the Qur'an, it becomes clear that the verse does not mention rivers, but rather "bodies of water," as reflected in the Arabic text (thanks to a Muslim friend for pointing this out):

- **Yusuf Ali**: "It is He Who has let free the two bodies of flowing water: One palatable and sweet, and the other salt and bitter; yet has He made a barrier between them, a partition that is forbidden to be passed."
- **Pickthal**: "And He it is Who hath given independence to the two seas (though they meet); one palatable, sweet, and the other saltish, bitter; and hath set a bar and a forbidding ban between them."
- **Shakir**: "And He it is Who has made two seas to flow freely, the one sweet that subdues thirst by its sweetness, and the other salt that burns by its saltness; and between the two He has made a barrier and inviolable obstruction."

In order to support a "modern scientific" interpretation, one must insist that one of these bodies of water is a river, and the other an ocean. Yet the Arabic text does not specify this distinction. Why does this matter? To interpret this verse in a way that aligns with modern science, one would need to assert that one body of water is a river (freshwater) and the other is an ocean (saltwater). Then, the concept of freshwater rivers flowing into oceans without mixing could be introduced. However, this interpretation overlooks a simpler reading:

1. The first "sea" or "body of water" (bahr) could refer to the Red Sea, known to Muhammad and salty in nature.
2. The second "sea" or "body of water" (bahr) could represent any local body of freshwater, such as an oasis.
3. These two "seas" or "bodies of water" are separated by land, creating an impassable barrier.
4. Thus, Sura 25:53 could be interpreted as a comment by Muhammad on the divine separation of fresh and saltwater.

This interpretation offers several advantages over the modern scientific explanation proposed by some:

i. **Historical Context**: If, as Suleiman claimed, Muhammad had never seen a river flow into the sea, then my interpretation fits better. In Muhammad's experience, fresh and saltwater were separate, as he would have known fresh water from oases and saltwater from the Red Sea.

ii. **Relevance Across Time**: This interpretation makes sense both in the 7th century when the verse was written and today. Early Muslims could understand it and praise Allah for His provision of fresh water, just as Muslims do now. The alternative interpretation, which requires the verse to have remained a mystery for over a millennium until modern science explained it, would suggest that the Qur'an was not relevant to all people at all times.

iii. **Purpose of the Verse**: Muhammad's mention of the separation between fresh and saltwater could simply reflect his understanding of the miraculous provision of fresh water, which he would have seen as a sign of Allah's mercy. This explanation is both understandable and meaningful, even without knowledge of modern science.

To support the "modern science proves the Qur'an" interpretation, one must reject this simpler, historical explanation in favor of a forced scientific reading, which relies on the assumption that the verse describes a miracle. However, this does not demonstrate that the Qur'an contains a scientific miracle; it merely suggests that one specific interpretation of the verse is "special" due to its alignment with modern science.

2) The Argument Makes Allah Appear Weak

If Allah intended to use science as proof of the Qur'an's divine origin, why not make it clear and undeniable? Instead of relying on complex interpretations, Allah could have provided a direct and unambiguous verse. For example, why not say something like: "Say: 'Men will watch images moving in a small box in their homes,'" referring to TV? Or,

"Say: 'Men will walk on the moon and plant a flag there,'" about the moon landings. Such verses would leave no room for debate, unlike the current situation, where supporters must engage in complicated interpretations and insist that their understanding is the only correct one, often disregarding centuries of scholarly interpretations.

Elsewhere in the Qur'an, when it speaks about something, it is crystal clear. Take, for instance, Sura 3:2:

"Allah! There is no god but He, the Living, the Self-Subsisting, Eternal." (Yusuf Ali)

There is no ambiguity here. This verse clearly affirms that Allah is the only god, living, self-sustaining, and eternal. If there were a scientific miracle in the Qur'an, it would serve as undeniable proof of its divine authorship. Yet this so-called miracle is hidden, requiring clever interpretations to uncover it. If Allah had intended science to be a sign in the Qur'an, it would have been written in an obvious and straightforward manner.

3) The Argument is a Modern Polemic

It is intriguing that the argument claiming "modern science proves the Qur'an" is a relatively recent one. Can anyone find a Muslim scholar putting forward this argument five hundred, two hundred, or even one hundred years ago? The answer is likely no. The reason for this is simple: the argument is a modern polemic. Science itself is not new, but this argument is. Why has it only emerged recently? Because, in recent times, people have started questioning the Qur'an rather than accepting it blindly. As a result, there has been a need to provide more "proof" of the Qur'an's divine authorship, especially to appeal to a scientific, Western mindset, as Islam seeks to make inroads in the West. Thus, this argument was born.

However, there is a problem with this approach: by tying the Qur'an to modern science, it risks making the Qur'an relevant only to a specific time period. If science is used as proof of the Qur'an's divinity, then in the future, Muslims will need to find new "scientific" miracles in the

Qur'an to remain consistent with modern knowledge. But science will continue to evolve, and the "modern" science that people are interpreting in the Qur'an today will likely be outdated. This leads to an interesting thought experiment:

- The Qur'an has about 6,400 verses.
- Let's assume, for argument's sake, that 10% of these verses can be interpreted to contain "science."
- This gives us 640 verses that could be cited as proof of scientific accuracy.

Now, let's say 20 new verses are being identified every year as containing scientific miracles. After 30 years, over 90% of these verses will have already been claimed. In less than five years, the pool of verses with potential "scientific miracles" will be exhausted. This means that in the future, people will look back at the Qur'an and see that its "scientific miracles" were relevant only between 1970 and 2002, and then the science stopped. This shows that the "modern science proves the Qur'an" argument is limited to a small timeframe and will soon run out of verses to use.

4) The Argument Uses Science to Judge the Qur'an, Not the Other Way Around

The debates over the meaning of Sura 18:86 in the soc.religion.islam newsgroup illustrate this point well. Here is the verse in question:

"Until, when he reached the setting of the sun, he found it set in a spring of murky water: Near it he found a People: We said: 'O Zulqarnain! (thou hast authority,) either to punish them, or to treat them with kindness.'" (Yusuf Ali)

No Muslim would claim that this verse was intended to describe a scientific fact. Why? Because, in the 21st century, we know that no one can physically reach the place where the sun sets. With modern technology, we can even "chase" or overtake the sunset. Furthermore, we know that the sun does not set in a body of water, let alone a muddy spring.

But here's the problem: when using this argument, Muslims are using science to judge the Qur'an. Those verses that seem to align with modern scientific understanding are declared miraculous, while those that appear to contradict it are said to be metaphorical or metaphysical. For example:

- **Sura 18:86**: Talks about someone finding the sunset, which contradicts science. Therefore, it is claimed to be metaphorical.
- **Sura 25:53**: Talks about two separate bodies of water, one sweet and one salty, which does not contradict science. Therefore, it is claimed to be scientifically accurate.

The issue is that by doing this, those who promote the "modern science proves the Qur'an" argument are contradicting a key tenet of Islam—that the Qur'an is the ultimate source of truth. By relying on science to validate the Qur'an, they are placing science as the judge of the Qur'an's truth.

5) Selective Interpretation Can Be Used to Prove Anything

As I mentioned in point 4, the "modern science proves the Qur'an" argument relies on selective interpretation. People pick verses that seem to support their point and ignore those that don't. This method can be used to prove anything. For example, imagine I wanted to convince people that I am a prophet who can predict the future. Let's say this was around the time of a major England vs. Scotland football match on November 14, 1999. Before the match, I made three predictions:

1. England will win.
2. Scotland will win.
3. It will be a draw.

After the match (which England won 2-0), I could say: "The second and third predictions were metaphorical, not meant to be taken literally. But the first prediction was a true statement. Therefore, I am a prophet!" It's clear this reasoning doesn't make sense. But people who argue that "modern science proves the Qur'an" use the same type of logic. When shown verses in the Qur'an that seem to contradict science (like Sura 18:86, which I often point out), they claim: "It's just a story," "It's metaphorical," or something else to explain away the contradiction. In proper interpretation, you can't use the outcome to justify the method.

6) Applying the Argument Means the Qur'an is No Longer Authoritative

If some Muslims argue that the Qur'an contains modern science and is therefore a miracle, there's a bigger problem. Their argument would mean that the Qur'an is no longer fully authoritative. For instance, let's say Sura 25:53 talks about ocean science, but it only provides a brief mention. To understand more, we would need to look outside the Qur'an—into scientific journals, books, and papers. This raises a critical question: if we need to turn to other sources to understand this topic more fully, why not do the same for other subjects in the Qur'an? How can Muslims say the Qur'an gives all the guidance people need for life? Do they need to read other texts to fully understand God's nature and how to live according to His will? If so, this undermines the Qur'an's authority.

Conclusion

No argument exists in isolation; there are always consequences to the position you take. This is true for the "modern science proves the Qur'an" argument. While it may sound appealing and neat in theory, if it were true, it would serve as proof of the Qur'an's divine origin. However, using this argument has severe logical consequences. It limits the Qur'an, diminishes God's role, elevates science above the Qur'an, and ultimately doesn't prove anything. Most importantly, it weakens the Qur'an's authority. As a method of argument, it is both weak and dangerous, and I believe Muslims should avoid it.

CHAPTER 2

Is the Quran's Ayats about the development Embryo Correct?

Professor Keith Moore, a renowned anatomist from the University of Toronto, Canada, was once struck by the remarkable accuracy of the Qur'an's descriptions of human embryonic development. As the author of a widely used embryology textbook in medical schools worldwide, Moore found the Qur'an's insights astonishing, especially given that they were recorded in the 7th century AD, long before the science of embryology existed. This discovery led many Muslim scholars to argue that the Qur'an contains knowledge about human development in the womb that could not have been known at the time of its revelation to Prophet Muhammad.

Recently, a book highlighted how this idea has been gaining more attention. Dubai's medical school introduced a compulsory course for all students called Islamic Medicine. This program connects modern medicine, including genetics, to the Qur'an. These courses have their roots in Saudi Arabia, where significant funds have been spent on medical conferences. At these conferences, prominent Western scientists are asked to confirm that certain Qur'anic verses, which may seem unclear to the average person, actually predict modern scientific ideas. These videos and pamphlets have been shared widely across the Muslim world by Saudi Arabia.

If it is true that certain verses in the Qur'an accurately describe scientific knowledge that couldn't have been known in the 7th century, it would suggest that the Qur'an must have had a divine author. This paper aims to examine what was actually known about human embryology during Muhammad's time to determine if the ideas in the Qur'an were accurate or well-known before that period.

The Origins of Life According to the Qur'an

There are at least 60 verses in the Qur'an that discuss human reproduction and development. These verses are spread throughout the Qur'an and many of the themes are repeated, which is common in the book. A good place to start is with what the Qur'an says about the material out of which humans are created. One might expect the Qur'an to be clear about such a basic topic, but the verses show there is considerable uncertainty about our origins. Unless stated otherwise, the translation used here is Yusuf Ali's (Saudi Revised Edition).

Were we made from earth?

- *11:61*: "It is He Who hath produced you from the earth."
- *15:26, 28, 33*: "We created man from sounding clay."
- *17:61*: "...Thou didst create from clay."
- *32:7*: "He began the creation of man from clay."

Were we made from nothing?

- *19:67*: "We created him before out of nothing."
- *52:35*: "Were they created of nothing?"

Were we made from mud?

- *23:12*: "We created man from a product of wet earth (loam)." (Pickthall)
- *23:12*: "Man We did create from a quintessence (of clay)."
- *38:71*: "I am about to create a mortal out of mire."

Were we made from water?

- *25:54*: "It is He Who has created man from water." (Also see 21:30, 24:45)

Were we made from dust?

- *3:59*: "He created (Jesus) out of dust."
- *30:20*: "He created you from dust."
- *35:11*: "Allah did create you from dust...."

Did we arise from the dead or from one person?

- *30:19*: "It is He who brings out the living from the dead."
- *39:6*: "He created you from a single Person." (Also see 4:1)

To address the ambiguity in these descriptions, some have suggested that all of the above verses are complementary, much like how a loaf of bread can be described as being made from dough, flour, carbohydrates, or molecules. However, this explanation avoids the core issue. The idea of God creating man from the dust of the earth is ancient and predates the Qur'an by thousands of years; it's found in the Bible in Genesis 2:7. If taken literally, this would contradict the theory of evolution, which claims that life originated from the oceans. Muslims, however, believe humans were created from both the oceans and the earth.

The Drop of Fluid or Semen

The Qur'an mentions in several places that man is created from a drop of fluid, often referring to semen, seed, or sperm. Here are some of the verses:

- *16:4*: "He created man from a drop of fluid." (Pickthall)
- *16:4*: "He has created man from a sperm-drop."
- *32:8*: "He made his seed from a quintessence of despised fluid."
- *35:11*: "... then from a little fluid." (Pickthall)
- *53:46*: "(he created) from a drop of seed when it is poured forth." (Pickthall)
- *53:46*: "From a sperm-drop when lodged (in its place)."
- *56:58*: "Have ye seen that which ye emit?" (Pickthall)
- *56:58*: "Do you then see? The (human seed) that ye emit."
- *75:37*: "Was he not a drop of fluid which gushed forth?" (Pickthall)
- *75:37*: "Was he not a drop of sperm emitted (in lowly form)?"
- *76:2*: "We create man from a drop of thickened fluid." (Pickthall)
- *76:2*: "We created man from a drop of mingled sperm."
- *77:20*: "Did We not create you from a worthless water?" (Al-Hilali & Khan)
- *80:19*: "From a sperm-drop He hath created him."
- *86:6-7*: "He is created from a drop emitted - proceeding from between the backbone and the ribs."

Could sixth-century Muslims have known about this? The fact that procreation involves the emission of a drop of fluid was already well known in ancient civilizations. For instance, in Genesis 38:9 of the Bible, Onan "spilled his semen on the ground to keep from producing offspring for his brother." The Qur'anic verses describing life originating from a drop of emitted fluid are simple observations of what happens during sexual intercourse. There's no need for divine revelation to inform us of this fact.

In the verses above, the Arabic word *nutfah* is used to describe the fluid released during intercourse, which clearly refers to semen. However, Professor Moore translates *nutfah* in Sura 76:2 as "mingled fluid," explaining that it refers to the male and female fluids containing gametes (sperm and egg). While the ancient Greeks couldn't see sperm or eggs as these were invisible without a microscope, the Qur'an doesn't specifically mention sperm or eggs. Instead, it simply says *nutfah*, which can reasonably be translated as semen, or in some cases, "germinal fluid," a term used by Hippocrates. If Moore insists on translating *nutfah* as germinal fluid, he inadvertently supports the idea that the Qur'an is drawing from Greek knowledge.

Sura 86:6 presents an interesting claim: it says that during intercourse, the "gushing fluid" (semen) comes from between the loins and ribs. This is problematic because we know that sperm is produced in the testicles, not around the kidneys or back. The ancient Greeks, like Aristotle, had strange ideas about reproduction, one of which was that sperm originated from the area around the kidneys and passed through the testicles. This idea, though clearly inaccurate, was well-known during Muhammad's time, which explains the erroneous description in the Qur'an.

Muslims often explain this apparent mistake by suggesting that the testicles, which produce sperm, originally developed from tissue in the area of the kidneys when the person was an embryo. This explanation, though complicated, aims to link the region of sperm production to the loins and ribs, where the testicles were believed to originate.

However, there's a simpler explanation. In the fifth century BC, Hippocrates and his followers believed that semen came from all the fluids in the body, starting in the brain and traveling through the spinal marrow, kidneys, and testicles before reaching the penis. This theory, though scientifically incorrect, was widely accepted at the time and could have influenced the Qur'an's description of semen coming from the loins.

It might be argued that the reference to "loins" in this verse is a metaphor. We see similar metaphorical usage in the Qur'an, such as in Sura 7:172 and 4:23, and in the Bible, where "loins" is used to describe descendants (e.g., Genesis 35:11 and 1 Kings 8:19). However, in Sura 86:6, the mention of "gushing fluid" and "ribs" refers to a physical process and seems to describe the mistaken ancient Greek belief about the origin of sperm. This is the first example we've found where an incorrect ancient Greek idea resurfaces in the Qur'an.

Embryological Development in the Qur'an

The Qur'an presents various stages of embryological development in several verses. In Sura 22:5, it states, "We created you out of dust, then out of sperm, then out of a leech-like clot, then from a morsel of flesh, partly formed and partly unformed... and We cause whom We will to rest in the wombs for an appointed term, then do We bring you out as babes." Sura 23:13-14 repeats this idea, explaining that God "placed him as (a drop of) sperm (nutfah) in a place of rest, firmly fixed; then We made the sperm into a clot of congealed blood (alaqa); then out of that clot We made a (foetus) lump (mudghah), then We made out of that lump bones and clothed the bones with flesh; then We developed out of it another creature." Similarly, Sura 75:38 mentions the alaqa stage, and Sura 96:2 says we came from alaq.

Professor Keith Moore, however, takes this further and claims in a later edition of his textbook that the Qur'an "states that the resulting organism settles in the womb like a seed, 6 days after its beginning." This would indeed be remarkable if true. However, the Qur'an does not state this, and Moore's claim does not align with the verses.

To determine whether the Qur'an contains scientifically accurate descriptions, we must examine the meaning of terms like *nutfah* and *alaqa*. The meaning of *nutfah* is clearer, referring to the sperm or semen. However, the term *alaqa* is more ambiguous. Various translations and interpretations exist: "clot" (Pickthall, Maulana Muhammed Ali), "small lump of blood" (Kasimirski), "leech-like clot" (Yusuf Ali), and "leech, suspended thing, or blood clot" (Moore). Moore suggests that a 24-day-old embryo resembles a leech, but this is debatable. At 24 days, the embryo is about 2 mm long, and it is difficult to reconcile the "leech-like" description with the embryo's actual appearance. In contrast, Hippocrates, in the 5th century BC, described the function of the umbilical cord, which "clings" to the uterus wall, an idea long before microscopes allowed scientists to see individual sperm and eggs.

The Arabic dictionary *Qamus al-Muheet* (compiled by Muhammed Ibn-Yaqub al-Firuzabadi in the 14th century) defines *alaqa* as "a clot of blood," which aligns with the common translation of *alaqa* as "clot" in the Qur'an. The term may also suggest "clinging" material, which could refer to the embryo's attachment to the uterus, but it is often interpreted as "clot" due to its singular form used in other verses. Early Muslim commentators like Ibn Kathir explained that the *nutfah* (sperm) becomes an *alaqa* (clot) after forty days in the womb, and then a *mudghah* (lump of flesh) after another forty days. This interpretation highlights the ambiguity of the Qur'anic description, which is more of a general observation rather than a precise scientific explanation.

Ibn Qayyim al-Jawziyya (about AD 1350) wrote that the foetus could sometimes be found in a slaughtered animal, its blood congested, which adds to the understanding of *alaqa* as a clot. Additionally, the physician Ibn al-Quff made significant contributions to embryology, noting that the embryo undergoes stages such as the *raghwah* stage (foam) about one week after conception, and that the embryo remains in the *alaqa* (clot) stage up to 16 days. After 27 to 30 days, the clot turns into a *mudghah*, a lump of meat.

Moving on to the *mudghah* stage, Razi described it as a little piece of meat, similar in size to what a man could chew. However, the term "chewed flesh" is a later, less accurate interpretation. The actual size of the embryo at 26-27 days is only about 4 mm long, far smaller than what could be described as a "mouthful" of flesh. By 80 days, the foetus is considerably larger, and its appearance no longer matches the description of "chewed flesh."

A Hadith transmitted by Bukhari and Muslim describes the embryonic development in three stages: sperm for 40 days, clot for another 40 days, and a lump of flesh for 40 days. However, human sperm only survives in the female reproductive tract for up to 7 days. By 80 days, the embryo has already developed into a recognizable human shape, and it is inaccurate to describe it as "chewed flesh" at this point.

In conclusion, while the Qur'an offers a description of embryological development, it is based on ancient observations and interpretations. The stages of development mentioned in the Qur'an are not scientifically precise and reflect the knowledge available at the time, rather than divinely revealed truths.

The Final Stages of Human Development in the Qur'an

The Qur'an describes the final stage of human development as the creation of bones and the clothing of those bones with flesh. However, modern embryologists, including Professor Moore, explain that the tissue from which both bones and muscles originate is the same, called the mesoderm. This means that bones and muscles actually develop at the same time, not sequentially. While most muscle tissue forms before birth, bones continue to develop and harden throughout the teenage years. The Qur'an's idea that bones are "clothed" with flesh is scientifically inaccurate. It would have been more accurate to say that muscles and bones begin developing together, but muscles complete their development earlier. This concept of bones being clothed with flesh is not only scientifically wrong but also mirrors an idea from the ancient Greek doctor Galen, as we will explore.

Ancient Ideas on Embryonic Development

In ancient Greek thought, Aristotle believed that human life began when male semen interacted with female menstrual blood. If we interpret the term *alaqa* in the Qur'an as "clot," this would make the Qur'an scientifically incorrect because there is no stage in human development where the embryo is a "clot." The only time an embryo might appear as a clot is during a miscarriage, where the blood is clotted and no longer alive. This might suggest that Muhammad, familiar with the occurrence of miscarriages, could have been influenced by such an observation. Alternatively, it might reflect Aristotle's mistaken belief about human development.

Professor Moore tries to avoid this issue by translating *alaqa* as a "leech," acknowledging that no stage in human development corresponds to a clot. However, this interpretation creates more problems. For instance, if *alaqa* is a "leech," implying the embryo clings to the uterus wall, this would suggest that the embryo only stays attached for a few days. But, as we know, the embryo stays attached for the entire pregnancy. Moore's interpretation also conflicts with Muhammad's timeline of embryonic stages, which is 40-80 days for *alaqa* and 80-120 days for *mudghah* (lump of flesh). These stages differ significantly from Moore's suggested 24-25 days and 26-27 days. Additionally, if the Qur'an offers a precise scientific account of human development, why does it only mention four stages: *nutfah*, *alaqa*, *mudghah*, and the creation of bones and flesh? Moore's textbook identifies 13 stages between fertilization and day 28. The lack of detail in the Qur'an raises questions about its scientific accuracy.

The Qur'an and Galenic Medicine

The most convincing explanation for the Qur'an's description of embryonic development is that it echoes the teachings of the Greek physician Galen. Galen, writing around AD 150, described the development of the embryo in four stages, which closely align with the stages mentioned in the Qur'an:

1. The first stage is when the semen prevails (similar to *nutfah* in the Qur'an).
2. The second stage is when the embryo is filled with blood and has the form of flesh but not yet the shape of organs (similar to *alaqa*).
3. The third stage is when the embryo takes on a form that can be recognized, resembling flesh but not fully developed (similar to *mudghah*).
4. The fourth and final stage is when all organs are formed, and the embryo moves, looking like a fully developed child.

This parallel between Galen's and the Qur'an's stages suggests that the Qur'an's descriptions are not scientifically revolutionary but rather reflect the ideas of ancient Greek medicine. Early Muslim doctors, including Ibn-Qayyim, recognized this similarity. As Basim Musallam, Director of the Centre of Middle Eastern Studies at the University of Cambridge, notes, "The stages of development which the Qur'an and Hadith established for believers agreed perfectly with Galen's scientific account."

Ancient Views on Embryology

It has been argued that the Qur'an's depiction of embryological stages anticipates modern science. However, many ancient cultures, including the Jewish Talmud, also described the development of the embryo in stages. For example, a 2nd-century Jewish physician named Samuel ha-Yehudi described six stages of embryonic development. These stages included terms like "golem" (formless) and "shefir meruqqam" (embroidered foetus), long before modern science provided its understanding.

With the knowledge available today, we understand that human development is a continuous process from conception to birth. This challenges the concept of discrete stages, as suggested in the Qur'an, and raises ethical debates around topics like abortion and embryo research. The idea that life begins in distinct stages, as the Qur'an suggests (Sura 71:14), doesn't align with the continuous nature of human development.

In conclusion, the Qur'an's depiction of embryological development aligns more closely with ancient Greek thought, particularly Galen's theories, than with modern scientific understanding. The Qur'an's stages of development reflect early medical knowledge, and its descriptions cannot be considered precise scientific insights.

More Examples of Borrowing from Ancient Greek Writers

Many of the ideas about embryology found in the Qur'an and Hadith can be traced back to ancient Greek writers. For example, there is a Hadith where Muhammad is asked why a group of red camels has a grey camel among them. He responds by explaining that it's due to a hidden trait. This idea closely resembles Aristotle's observation that babies who looked different from their parents often resembled their grandparents. He explained this as a recessive trait, where a characteristic skips a generation. Aristotle also described a woman from Elis who married a black man, and although their daughter wasn't black, their granddaughter was. This shows a gene skipping a generation in the same way Muhammad described in the Hadith.

Another Hadith explains how the sex of a child is determined by the dominance of either the male's or female's fluid. Some have tried to link this with modern genetics, but it actually repeats Hippocrates' mistaken belief that both men and women produce both male and female sperm. According to Hippocrates, the sex of the child was determined by which sperm was stronger or in greater quantity. He claimed that if both parents produced "strong sperm," a male child would result, and if "weak sperm" predominated, a female child would be conceived. This is not a scientific explanation but reflects outdated Greek theories.

In the same Hadith, Muhammad describes the male reproductive fluid as white and the female's as yellow, which resembles the contents of chick eggs, something Aristotle was known to study. The Hadith goes on to say that an angel is sent by Allah to shape the embryo and ask its sex. While modern science knows that the sex of a child is determined by chromosomes at the moment of conception, Hippocrates believed that it took 30 days for male genitals to form and 42 days for female genitals. This aligns with Muhammad's teaching that the angel appears after 40 or 50 days, though the truth is that the external genitalia only begin to differentiate around 9 weeks of gestation.

Sura 39:6 says God created us in stages, in threefold darkness. Some interpretations suggest these three stages refer to three membranes surrounding the fetus: one for nutrients, one for waste, and one for urine. This is based on observable anatomy, similar to what Hippocrates described after dissecting pregnant animals. The Romans even practiced opening the womb of deceased pregnant women to remove the fetus, which is where the term "Caesarean section" originated.

Sura 80:20 claims that Allah makes childbirth easy, but this contradicts Sura 46:15, which says that a mother bears her child with difficulty. In reality, childbirth is one of the most dangerous experiences a woman can face, with high maternal mortality rates in many parts of the world. The Biblical account of childbirth being painful (Genesis 3:16) is more realistic.

Sura 46:15 says the duration of pregnancy and weaning is thirty months, which implies a normal pregnancy lasts six months. However, with modern technology, babies born at 24 weeks gestation may survive, but with severe disabilities. The Qur'an's description of pregnancy duration is inaccurate for the time, as no babies could survive at such a premature stage in Muhammad's day.

Sura 33:4 mentions that Allah hasn't put two hearts in a man, though there are historical records of people born with two hearts. This was noted by famous anatomists, showing that the Qur'an is not scientifically accurate in this regard.

The Qur'an also contains commands that seem advanced but were actually known by ancient civilizations. For example, Sura 2:222 tells Muhammad that menstruation is an illness and that men should avoid sexual intercourse with their wives during this time. However, the command in the Torah (Leviticus 18:19) prohibiting sex during menstruation was not for health reasons, but for religious purposes. Contrary to some modern claims, menstruation is not an illness; it's a natural process that actually helps reduce the risk of uterine cancer.

How Could Muhammad Have Known These Things?

It's one thing to see that the Qur'an repeats ideas about embryology that were first described by ancient Greeks, but how can we be sure that the people of Muhammad's time knew about these ideas? The key lies in the influence of Greek medical knowledge, especially the work of Galen. Around the sixth century AD, a Christian priest named Sergius of Resh'Aina translated about 26 books of Galen's work into Syriac. Sergius studied medicine in Alexandria and worked in Mesopotamia, and his translations were part of a larger effort by Nestorian Christians to spread Greek medical knowledge. These translations were used in many learning centers, including the famous Jundishapur medical school in Persia, which became a major hub for knowledge.

Jundishapur was founded in AD 555 during the reign of the Persian king Chosroes the Great. At its peak, it was a thriving center of medical learning that brought together Greek, Indian, and Persian medical traditions. This school played a crucial role in passing down Greek medical knowledge to the Arab world. In fact, when the Arabs entered Persia, they encountered these Syriac translations and benefited from them in their own medical studies.

One of the most famous graduates of Jundishapur was Harith Ibn Kalada, a doctor who lived around the same time as Muhammad. Harith studied at Jundishapur and became familiar with the teachings of famous Greek physicians like Hippocrates, Aristotle, and Galen. He later returned to Mecca, where he became the leading physician among the Arabs. It's even said that Muhammad sought medical advice from Harith Ibn Kalada. Some historians suggest that Harith influenced Muhammad's knowledge of medicine, and it's possible that he shared Greek medical knowledge with Muhammad.

Harith Ibn Kalada was not only a doctor but also adopted a man named Harith al-Nasar (Nadr), who was Muhammad's cousin. Nadr, however, mocked Muhammad's teachings and claimed that the stories in the Qur'an were less impressive than the Persian legends he had heard. This made him an enemy of Muhammad, and he was eventually killed after being captured in the Battle of Badr.

So, there's a clear link that shows how Greek medical knowledge from Galen was passed through Syriac translations and influenced the knowledge that Muhammad may have had. As a summary, we can say that by the time of Muhammad, Greek medical writings, especially those of Galen, had been translated into Syriac and were available in places like Jundishapur. Harith Ibn Kalada, who studied in Jundishapur and later became a companion of Muhammad, likely shared this knowledge, allowing traces of Greek medical ideas to appear in the Qur'an.

How Much of the Qur'an Comes from Human Sources?

There's a story in Muslim traditions that suggests at least one verse in the Qur'an about human development was influenced by human input. While Muhammad was dictating verse 23:14 to Abdullah Ibn Abi

Sarh, Abdullah became so moved by the description of human creation that he added the words, "Blessed be God, the best of creators!" when Muhammad reached the phrase "another creature." Muhammad accepted these words as part of the revelation and asked Abdullah to write them down, even though they were clearly Abdullah's words, not Muhammad's or Allah's.

This raises an important question: if one verse in the Qur'an contains words added by a human, how can we be sure that this didn't happen in other parts of the Qur'an?

After the fall of Alexandria in AD 642, Greek medical knowledge spread quickly throughout the Arab world. In the 9th century, Hunain Ibn Ishaq made significant Arabic translations of Hippocrates and Galen's works. Additionally, the philosopher and physician al-Kindi wrote more than twenty medical treatises, including one specifically on Hippocrates.

Arabic medical writers acknowledged the influence of Greek and Indian medical traditions. For example, in about AD 850, Ali at-Tabari, a Christian convert to Islam, wrote a medical work called *Paradise of Wisdom* in Samarra, Mesopotamia. In it, he stated that he was following the methods of Hippocrates and Aristotle. The book includes a chapter on the genesis of the embryo, which mirrors the ideas of Aristotle, specifically that the embryo forms from the mixing of sperm and menstrual blood. The historian Arthur Meyer noted that at-Tabari's work relied heavily on Greek sources, implying that there was little independent Arabic knowledge in this area at the time.

Ibn Qayyim al-Jawziyya, a medieval philosopher, also relied heavily on Greek medical teachings. In one of his writings, he used the ideas of Hippocrates to explain both the Qur'an and the Hadith, and vice versa. For example, he discussed how Hippocrates described the formation of membranes during pregnancy, and he linked this to the Qur'anic verse about creation in the "three darknesses" of the womb. He also referenced how Hippocrates described the development of the ears and eyes in the embryo, which aligned with sayings from the

Prophet Muhammad. In this way, Ibn Qayyim mixed Greek teachings, Qur'anic verses, Hadith, and his own thoughts in a single discourse.

Throughout the time of Muhammad, people were familiar with both Greek and Indian medicine, and many medical ideas from these cultures were incorporated into later Arabic medical writings.

Other notable figures in early Arabic medicine, such as Abu Ali al-Hasan Ibn Sina, who lived from AD 980-1037 and wrote the *Canon of Medicine*, didn't add new ideas to what Galen had already written. Greek thinkers like Clement of Alexandria and Lactantius of Nicomedia also shared similar beliefs about the formation of the embryo, often stating that it resulted from the combination of semen and menstrual blood.

How Much of the Qur'an Comes from Human Sources?

There's a story in Muslim traditions that suggests at least one verse in the Qur'an about human development was influenced by human input. While Muhammad was dictating verse 23:14 to Abdullah Ibn Abi Sarh, Abdullah became so moved by the description of human creation that he added the words, "Blessed be God, the best of creators!" when Muhammad reached the phrase "another creature." Muhammad accepted these words as part of the revelation and asked Abdullah to write them down, even though they were clearly Abdullah's words, not Muhammad's or Allah's.

This raises an important question: if one verse in the Qur'an contains words added by a human, how can we be sure that this didn't happen in other parts of the Qur'an?

After the fall of Alexandria in AD 642, Greek medical knowledge spread quickly throughout the Arab world. In the 9th century, Hunain Ibn Ishaq made significant Arabic translations of Hippocrates and Galen's works. Additionally, the philosopher and physician al-Kindi wrote more than twenty medical treatises, including one specifically on Hippocrates.

Arabic medical writers acknowledged the influence of Greek and Indian medical traditions. For example, in about AD 850, Ali at-Tabari, a Christian convert to Islam, wrote a medical work called *Paradise of Wisdom* in Samarra, Mesopotamia. In it, he stated that he was following the methods of Hippocrates and Aristotle. The book includes a chapter on the genesis of the embryo, which mirrors the ideas of Aristotle, specifically that the embryo forms from the mixing of sperm and menstrual blood. The historian Arthur Meyer noted that at-Tabari's work relied heavily on Greek sources, implying that there was little independent Arabic knowledge in this area at the time.

Ibn Qayyim al-Jawziyya, a medieval philosopher, also relied heavily on Greek medical teachings. In one of his writings, he used the ideas of Hippocrates to explain both the Qur'an and the Hadith, and vice versa. For example, he discussed how Hippocrates described the formation of membranes during pregnancy, and he linked this to the Qur'anic verse about creation in the "three darknesses" of the womb. He also referenced how Hippocrates described the development of the ears and eyes in the embryo, which aligned with sayings from the Prophet Muhammad. In this way, Ibn Qayyim mixed Greek teachings, Qur'anic verses, Hadith, and his own thoughts in a single discourse.

Throughout the time of Muhammad, people were familiar with both Greek and Indian medicine, and many medical ideas from these cultures were incorporated into later Arabic medical writings.

Other notable figures in early Arabic medicine, such as Abu Ali al-Hasan Ibn Sina, who lived from AD 980-1037 and wrote the *Canon of Medicine*, didn't add new ideas to what Galen had already written. Greek thinkers like Clement of Alexandria and Lactantius of Nicomedia also shared similar beliefs about the formation of the embryo, often stating that it resulted from the combination of semen and menstrual blood.

How Could Muhammad Have Known These Things?

It seems that even Professor Moore is not fully convinced by the scientific claims in the Qur'an. The Islamic edition of his textbook, which includes additions related to Islamic teachings, is not available in major libraries like the British Library or the US Library of Congress. This is likely because Professor Moore understands that the Islamic additions contradict both modern science and his own textbook. In fact, in the bibliography for his textbook, Moore refers to J. Needham's work on the history of embryology. Needham, however, dismisses the Arabic claims about embryology, saying they are just a "seventh-century echo of Aristotle and the Ayer-veda"—basically a mix of Greek and ancient Indian ideas.

In the most recent edition of Moore's textbook, he also references Basim Musallam's work, which highlights the similarities between the Qur'anic view of embryology and the ideas of Galen, and how ancient Muslim scholars never questioned this link.

To conclude, none of the embryological statements in the Qur'an that relate to modern science were new or unknown to ancient Greek and Indian doctors. Many of these ideas were well known through direct observation long before the Qur'an was written. The Greek medical texts had been translated into Syriac even before Muhammad's time, making them accessible to non-Greek speakers. We also know that one of Muhammad's companions, Harith Ibn Kalada, trained at the medical school in Jundishapur, where these Greek translations were used. Additionally, at least one verse in the Qur'an, Sura 23:14, contains words added by Muhammad's companion, Abdullah Ibn Abi Sarh. This suggests that, rather than providing divine insight, the Qur'an's embryological statements are based on human knowledge from earlier traditions.

Thus, far from proving the Qur'an's divine origin, its embryological content provides further evidence of human influence.

CHAPTER 3

Alaqa "Clot" and Other Embryological Stages in the Quran

Some have claimed that the Qur'an describes the development of the embryo in stages, predicting modern embryology. In a pamphlet titled *Highlights of Human Embryology in the Koran and the Hadith*, Dr. Keith Moore suggests that the idea of the embryo developing in stages wasn't discussed until the 15th century AD. He also claims that the stages in the Qur'an align with modern knowledge. But, let's look at the actual meanings of the Arabic words used in the Qur'an and the historical context to evaluate these claims.

The Word 'ALAQA

The Arabic word *'alaqa* is used in six places across five verses in the Qur'an to describe a stage in the development of the fetus.

In Sura 75:37-39, we read: "Was he (man) not a drop of sperm ejaculated? Then he became a leech-like clot (*'alaqa*) and God shaped and formed and made of him a pair, the male and the female."

In Sura 40:67: "He it is Who created you from dust, then from a sperm-drop, then from a leech-like clot (*'alaqa*), then brings you forth as a child, ... that perhaps you may understand."

In Sura 22:5: "O mankind! if you have doubt about the resurrection (consider) that We have created you from dust, then from a drop of seed, then from a clot (*'alaqa*), then from a little lump of flesh, shapely and shapeless ..."

And in Sura 23:12-14: "Verily We created man from a product of wet earth, then placed him as a drop of seed in a safe lodging, then We fashioned the drop a clot (*'alaqa*), and of the clot (*'alaqa*) We fashioned a lump, and of the lump We fashioned bones, and We clothed the bones (with) meat. Then We produced it as another creation."

The Stages of Prenatal Development in the Qur'an

1. **Nutfah** – Sperm
2. **'Alaqa** – Clot
3. **Mudghah** – Lump of flesh
4. **'Adaam** – Bones
5. **Clothing the bones with muscles**

Translation Issues

Over the past century, the word *'alaqa* has been translated in various ways:

- French: "un grumeau de sang" (a small lump of blood)
- "A leech-like clot" – Yusuf Ali (1938), 1946
- "A clot" – Pickthall (1940), 1977
- "A clot of blood" – N. J. Dawood (1980)

- Indonesian: "segumpal darah" (lump of blood)
- Chinese: "xue kuai" (blood clot)

As anyone who has studied human reproduction knows, there is no stage in fetal development where the embryo is simply a "clot." This presents a major scientific issue.

The Meaning of *'Alaqa*

In the dictionaries of Wehr and Abdel-Nour, *'alaqa* is defined as either "clot" or "leech," and these meanings are still commonly used in North Africa. Many patients have come to me asking to have a "leech" removed from their throats, and some women, believing the fetus goes through a "clot" stage, have asked for medicine when their periods are late. When I explain that I believe the fetus is already a person, they often respond, "But it's still blood."

This suggests that the term *'alaqa* in the Qur'an is problematic, as it implies a stage in fetal development that doesn't exist scientifically.

The first verses that Muhammad received in Mecca are in the 96th Sura, called *'Alaq* (Clots?), from the very word we are discussing. In verses 96:1-2, we read:

"Proclaim! In the name of your Lord who created—created man from 'alaq."

Here, the word *'alaq* is in the collective plural form. This form can have multiple meanings because *'alaq* is also derived from the verb *'aliqa*, which means "to hang, be suspended, dangle, to stick, cling, cleave, adhere, and to be attached." The verbal noun typically corresponds to the gerund in English, as in the sentence "Swimming is fun." Therefore, it can mean hanging, clinging, adhering, etc. Additionally, the verbal noun can have other meanings based on how it is used.

However, the twelve translators mentioned above have all considered this to be the collective plural of *'alaqa*, translating it as "clot" or "congealed blood" in this verse. Fazlur Rahman also uses "congealed blood" in his well-known book *Islam*, first published in 1966.

Maulana Muhammad Ali provides an explanation for this translation in Note 2770. He says:

"*'Alaq* signifies both a clot of blood and attachment or love. The clot interpretation is generally accepted because of its mention in other parts of the Qur'an in reference to the creation of man, indicating the humble origin of humanity."

In other words, the singular form of *'alaqa* is influencing the plural form, despite the fact that there is an attraction to use a different word to avoid scientific difficulties.

Despite the number and qualifications of translators who use the word "clot" to translate *'alaqa*, the French doctor Maurice Bucaille has strong words for them. He writes:

"What is more likely to mislead the reader is, once again, the problem of vocabulary... The majority of translations describe, for example, man's formation from a 'blood clot' or 'adhesion.' This is completely unacceptable to scientists specializing in this field... This highlights the importance of combining linguistic and scientific knowledge when interpreting the Qur'anic statements on reproduction."

In other words, according to Bucaille, "No one has translated the Qur'an correctly until he came along."

So, how does Dr. Bucaille think this word should be translated? He suggests that instead of "clot," *'alaqa* should be translated as "something that clings," referring to the fetus being attached to the uterus through the placenta.

Let's try this translation and apply it:

"Then from the sperm-drop We created (or fashioned) the thing which clings, and from the thing which clings We created (or fashioned) chewed flesh, and from the chewed flesh We created (or fashioned) bones, and We clothed the bones with meat."

Now, with this modern approach, where is the ovum? "The thing which clings" is not formed from a sperm-drop. It forms when the sperm and egg (ovum) fuse. Leaving out the ovum is not technically an error, but we'll see later that in the context of Muhammad's time, *'alaqa* was understood to be the female contribution.

Additionally, "the thing which clings" doesn't stop clinging to become "chewed flesh." The fetus remains attached via the placenta throughout the pregnancy, not transforming into "chewed meat."

Even among scientists, there is disagreement about the translation of *'alaqa*. Dr. Bechir Torki offers another solution, translating Sura 96 as:

"Read in the name of your Lord Who has created, who has created man from links (d'attaches). Read, for your Lord is most generous. It is He Who has taught by the pen."

The French word *links* (which can mean bonds, ties, or attachments) sounds similar to Bucaille's interpretation, but Torki suggests a very different understanding. He writes:

"He (God) 'created man from links (or bonds)'... in which all the genes of the cells are attached or suspended... The first 'read' in the Sura refers to the information in the first cell that forms the structure of man, and the second 'read' refers to the Qur'an, which God has taught to man by the pen."

While this is an interesting interpretation, it's hard to believe that God's first words to Muhammad would be "Read the gene code." What would the people of Mecca have understood? Moreover, what does Torki do with other verses where *'alaqa* is used? What does it mean, even with modern education, to say, "From a drop of sperm we created 'a gene code'; and from 'a gene code' we created a lump of flesh"? The gene code is in the sperm, not created from it.

Translation of 'ALAQA and Embryological Stages in the Qur'an

Some translators have used different words to translate *'alaqa*. In his 1957 translation, Regis Blachère renders Sura 23:14 as:

"We have made the ejaculation an adhesion, We have made the adhesion a flabby mass. We have made of the flabby mass a skeleton, and we have clothed the skeleton with flesh."

However, it's worth noting that in Sura 75:38, Blachère translates it as "a congealed drop."

Muhammad Asad, in his 1964 translation (published in 1980), suggests:

"And then We created out of the drop of sperm a germ-cell, and then We created out of the germ-cell an embryonic lump, and then we created within the embryonic lump bones, and then we clothed the bones with flesh."

Asad also notes that *'alaqa* refers to the fertilized ovum, suggesting it means "germ-cell."

However, it's clear that:

(a) The sperm cannot become an adhesion or a fertilized ovum without the unfertilized female ovum. (b) To say *'alaqa* means "germ-cell" or "fertilized ovum" is an assumption. (c) If it is an adhesion, it stays stuck throughout the pregnancy and does not change. (d) Translating "mudghah" (lump of flesh) as "embryonic" and saying the bones are created "within" the embryonic lump instead of "from" it, are also assumptions.

Dr. Keith Moore's View on 'ALAQA

Dr. Keith Moore, a retired professor of anatomy and author of a textbook on embryology, suggests that one verse in the Qur'an refers to the leech-like appearance and chewed stages of human development. Dr. Moore proposes that a 23-day-old embryo, about 3 mm long, resembles a leech. This is based on Carnegie stage 10, as shown in his textbook.

However, an x-ray image of the embryo at day 22-23 shows the neural groove and other features that do not resemble a leech. A leech does not have these characteristics, such as the large ventral yolk sac and umbilical stalk present in the embryo.

In conclusion, a 23-day-old embryo does not look like a leech at all. Furthermore, no dictionary defines *‘alaqa* as "leech-like." Dr. Moore, who does not speak Arabic, even admitted in a personal conversation that if *‘alaqa* means "clot," then there is no such stage in embryonic development.

‘ADAAM — BONES BEFORE MUSCLE

The Qur'anic verses suggest that the "lump of flesh" becomes bones, and then the bones are covered with muscles. This idea is repeated in Sura 2:259:

"... Look further at the bones, how We bring them together and clothe them with flesh..."

This implies that bones form first, and then flesh is added. Dr. Bucaille points out that this is not scientifically accurate.

Muscles and the cartilage precursors of bones begin developing at the same time from the somite. By the end of the eighth week, some ossification (bone formation) has started, and the fetus is already capable of some movement. Dr. T.W. Sadler, an anatomy professor, confirms this in a letter, stating that by the 8th week, the ribs are cartilaginous and muscles are already present, with ossification beginning near the ribs. By weeks 10-12, muscle movement becomes much more developed.

Dr. Keith Moore also provides details in his textbook *The Developing Human*. He explains that both the skeletal and muscle systems develop from mesoderm cells, which can differentiate into osteoblasts (bone-forming cells) and muscles. Initially, bones form as cartilage models, and by the end of the sixth week, the entire limb skeleton is cartilage, without calcium deposits.

In conclusion, the Qur'an's depiction of bone and muscle formation does not align with modern embryology, where bones and muscles develop simultaneously, rather than in separate stages.

Embryology in the Qur'an: Understanding the Stages and the Problem

Bone and Muscle Development

During the development of bones, myoblasts (cells that develop into muscle tissue) form a large muscle mass in each limb bud, dividing into components for extension and flexion. In simpler terms, muscle development happens at the same time as the bones form, both from the mesenchyme, a type of connective tissue around the bones. Dr. Moore agrees with Dr. Sadler on this process.

When I discussed Dr. Sadler's statement with Dr. Moore, he confirmed that it was absolutely accurate.

Conclusion on Bone Development

Both Dr. Sadler and Dr. Moore agree: there is no point when calcified bones form first, with muscles added around them afterward. In reality, muscles begin to form before bones are calcified. The Qur'an's description of bones being formed first and then covered with muscles is scientifically incorrect.

The Problem with Modern Definitions of *'ALAQA* and *MUDGHA*

The issue with the modern definitions of *'alaqa* (translated as "clot") and *mudghah* (translated as "lump of flesh") is that no examples of these meanings have been found in the Arabic used around the time of the Qur'an's revelation.

Dr. Maurice Bucaille claims that older translations are wrong and that a good understanding of science is needed for accurate translation. However, these translators were experts in their field of language and have not found any valid linguistic support for changing the meaning of these words. They were honest translators, not unaware of science.

Dr. Bucaille argues that their translations are "hardly comprehensible," but I disagree. Their translations are clear and accurate, reflecting the scientific limitations of the original Arabic text.

The Importance of Language Usage

The meaning of a word can only be established by its usage in the language. To determine whether *'alaqa* can mean a 3mm embryo or "the thing that clings," we need to examine examples from the literature of the Arabs of Mecca and Medina at the time of Muhammad, especially the language of the Quraish tribe. The Qur'an was written in "Clear Arabic," the colloquial Arabic of the Quraish.

The early Muslim scholars understood the importance of accurately interpreting the Qur'anic words, and they made extensive studies of their language. The famous historian Ibn Khaldun said, "The Qur'an descended in the language of the Arabs, and all of them understood it and knew its meanings."

Hamza Boubakeur, former rector of the main mosque in Paris, also noted that ancient poetry demonstrates the stability of meanings over time. If the Qur'an's spiritual messages have remained stable, the scientific aspects should be accepted as stable unless new evidence arises.

The Question: What Did the People of Mecca Understand?

Some verses in the Qur'an state that the creation of man is a "sign." For example, Sura 40:76 says, "He it is Who created you from dust, then from a sperm-drop, then from a clot ('alaqa) ... that perhaps you may understand." Similarly, Sura 22:5 says, "O mankind! If you have doubt about the resurrection, consider that We have created you from dust..."

This raises an important question: What did the people of Mecca and Medina understand from the word *'alaqa* that led them to believe in the resurrection?

The Answer: Historical Context

To understand the beliefs about embryology during Muhammad's time, we need to look at the medical knowledge from Greek and Indian scholars, starting with Hippocrates.

Hippocrates' Stages of Embryology

Hippocrates, who lived around 460 BC on the Greek island of Cos, described the following stages of human development:

1. **Semen**: Sperm comes from the entire body of each parent, with stronger sperm coming from stronger parts of the body.
2. **Coagulation of Mother's Blood**: The embryo forms in a membrane, growing from the mother's blood. After conception, a woman stops menstruating.
3. **Flesh**: As the blood coagulates, flesh begins to form, and the umbilical cord develops.
4. **Bones**: The flesh forms distinct limbs, and the bones become hard. The bones grow and branch like tree limbs.

These stages, as described by Hippocrates, align with the knowledge of human development known at the time. This information was influential during the time of Muhammad and provides the context for understanding the embryology mentioned in the Qur'an.

Stages of Prenatal Development According to Hippocrates

Stage 1: Sperm
Stage 2: Mother's blood descends around the membrane
Stage 3: Flesh, fed through the umbilicus
Stage 4: Bones

This clearly shows that, over 1,000 years before the Qur'an, the development of the embryo was already understood to occur in stages.

Aristotle's View on Embryology

Aristotle, in his work *On the Generation of Animals* (around 350 BC), described the stages of embryology as follows:

1. **Semen and Menstrual Blood**: Aristotle believed that male semen and female menstrual blood combined to form the embryo. The male semen worked on the female's menstrual blood.
2. **Flesh**: The purest material from the semen forms the flesh.
3. **Bones**: The flesh is then formed into bones.
4. **Flesh Around the Bones**: Finally, the fleshy parts grow around the bones, attaching to them with fibrous bands.

This sequence is remarkably similar to the Qur'anic description of embryological development.

Stages of Prenatal Development According to Aristotle

Stage 1: Sperm
Stage 2: Menstrual blood (catamenia)
Stage 3: Flesh
Stage 4: Bones
Stage 5: Flesh grows around the bones

Indian Medicine's View on Embryology

In Indian medicine, both Charaka (123 AD) and Susruta agreed that both the male and female contributed to the creation of a child. The male's "secretion" is called *sukra* (semen), and the female's "secretion" is called *artava* or *sonita* (blood), derived from food and transformed into blood. This also aligns with the idea that the embryo is formed from male semen and female menstrual blood.

Galen's View on Embryology

Galen, born in 131 AD in Pergamum (modern-day Bergama, Turkey), contributed significantly to our understanding of embryology. His work, *De Semine*, was influential, and though the original manuscripts were lost, the Arabic translations from the 12th and 13th centuries remain accurate.

Galen believed that the fetus is formed from a mixture of menstrual blood and two types of semen—male and female. This concept is reflected in the Qur'an in Sura 76:2, which says, "We created man from a drop of mingled sperm."

Embryological Development According to Galen

1. **First Stage**: The form of the semen prevails, and it is still considered semen.
2. **Second Stage**: The embryo fills with blood, and the heart, brain, and liver are not yet shaped. Galen referred to this stage as the "foetus."
3. **Third Stage**: Flesh grows around the bones, as described in Sura 23:14 of the Qur'an, which says, "And we clothed the bones with meat."
4. **Fourth Stage**: The embryo reaches a stage where all the parts of the body are differentiated and fully formed.

This process is very similar to the stages of development described in the Qur'an and shows how the Qur'an's embryological statements are in line with the scientific views of the time, as understood by Hippocrates, Aristotle, and Galen.

Galen's Stages of Prenatal Development

Stage 1: The two types of semen
Stage 1b: Plus menstrual blood
Stage 2: Unshaped flesh
Stage 3: Bones
Stage 3b: Flesh grows on and around the bones

This shows that, although Galen divides the stages differently, the overall sequence is quite similar to other descriptions.

Galen's Influence on Medical Studies

Galen's works were so important in medicine that around the time of the Hijra (the migration of Muhammad and his followers), four leading medical scholars in Alexandria, Egypt, formed a medical school using Galen's *16 books* as their foundation. This practice continued well into the 13th century.

Arabia Around 600 AD: The Medical Context

At the time of Muhammad, the Arabian Peninsula was a center for trade, connecting Africa, the Middle East, and parts of Europe. Caravans carrying goods like spices passed through Mecca and Medina, which had exposure to various medical traditions. For instance, the Ghassanid Arabs controlled parts of the Syrian desert by the 6th century and used Syriac, a language related to Arabic.

Syriac Translations and Medical Knowledge:

- By 463 AD, the Torah and Old Testament were translated from Hebrew into Syriac.
- Notably, a key figure, **Sergius of Ras Ayni**, translated 26 books of Galen's works into Syriac around 536 AD, making Greek medical knowledge available in the region.
- **Khosru I**, the King of Persia (531–579 AD), was passionate about education and founded the medical school at Jundi-

Shapur, which became a significant intellectual center during his reign. There, Greek, Jewish, Persian, and Hindu knowledge merged, and many Greek medical texts were translated into Syriac.

Local Medical Expertise in Muhammad's Time

Physicians in Arabia during Muhammad's time were familiar with Greek medical knowledge. One prominent example is **Harith ben Kalada**, who studied medicine at Jundi-Shapur and was trained in the teachings of Aristotle, Hippocrates, and Galen. He later returned to Arabia, where he became a well-known physician.

- Harith ben Kalada treated King Abu'l-Khayr of Yemen, who rewarded him after being cured.
- Muhammad occasionally sent patients to Harith for treatment, which further links Muhammad's community to Greek medicine.

Other Key Figures

Nadr ben Harith, a cousin of Muhammad, also visited Khosru's court. He learned Persian and even introduced Persian music to the Quraish in Mecca. However, he mocked Muhammad's teachings, and Muhammad had him executed after he was captured in the Battle of Badr.

Key Points:

1. Arabs in Mecca and Medina had political and economic ties with regions like Ethiopia, Yemen, Persia, and Byzantium.
2. Muhammad's cousin knew Persian and studied music, showing his exposure to foreign cultures.
3. The Ghassanid tribe, with ties to Mecca, used Syriac, which was also the language used at Jundi-Shapur for teaching medicine.

4. Harith ben Kalada, a physician trained at Jundi-Shapur, practiced medicine in Arabia, showing direct contact with Greek medical knowledge.
5. During Muhammad's lifetime, medical schools in Alexandria used Galen's 16 books for their curriculum.

Conclusion: Exposure to Greek Medical Theories

Given the connections to Jundi-Shapur and the medical schools around Muhammad's time, it is likely that the people in Mecca and Medina had heard of the embryological theories of Aristotle, Hippocrates, and Galen. These ideas may have influenced the Qur'anic descriptions of embryological development, particularly in verses like:

- **Sura 40:67 (The Believer)**: "He it is Who created you from dust, then from a sperm-drop, then from a leech-like clot ('alaqa) ... that perhaps you may understand."
- **Sura 22:5 (The Pilgrimage)**: "O mankind! If you have doubt about the resurrection (consider) that We have created you from dust, then from a drop of seed, then from a clot ('alaqa), etc."

This raises the question: what did the people of Mecca and Medina understand from the word 'alaqa that would lead them to believe in the resurrection and creation? It is likely they understood it in a way that fit with the medical knowledge they had at the time, which was largely influenced by Greek medical traditions.

Quranic Stages of Prenatal Development

1. **Stage 1:** Nutfa – sperm
2. **Stage 2:** 'Alaqa – clot
3. **Stage 3:** Mudagha – piece or lump of flesh
4. **Stage 4:** Adaam – bones
5. **Stage 5:** Dressing the bones with muscles

These stages reflect the common knowledge of embryology at the time, mainly based on teachings from Greek physicians. While the names of the Greek physicians were not necessarily known to Muhammad's listeners, the general concepts were understood:

1. They believed that male sperm mixed with female semen and menstrual blood to form the baby.
2. They thought the fetus first appeared as a clot, then a lump.
3. They understood that the lump developed into bones.
4. These bones were then covered with muscles.

Allah in the Qur'an used this common knowledge as a sign to encourage the listeners to turn to Him. However, the problem is that this knowledge was scientifically incorrect then and still is today.

Arab Physicians After Muhammad

Even after Muhammad, the ideas of embryology, as taught by Greek physicians like Aristotle, Hippocrates, and Galen, continued to influence Arab physicians well into the 1600s.

Hadith: One example is a Hadith found in the "Forty Hadiths" of An-Nawawi, which recounts a teaching of Muhammad:

- **Hadith from Abi 'Abd-ar-rahman 'Abdallah ben Mas'ud**: The Prophet Muhammad said that the creation of every person occurs in various stages in the mother's womb. First, the sperm stays for 40 days, then it becomes a clot ('alaqa) for 40 days, followed by "chewed meat" (mudagha) for another 40 days. After this, an angel is sent to breathe life into the fetus and record the person's future, including their fortune, lifespan, actions, and ultimate fate.

The Hadith mirrors the stages described in the Qur'an but adds extra details. Modern science shows that sperm only survives inside the female body for about a week, and organ development begins much earlier than the 70-80 days indicated in the Hadith. By day 70, organ differentiation, except for the brain, is already well-advanced.

Scientific Error in the Hadith:

- The sperm doesn't stay in the female body for 40 days, as the Hadith suggests.
- Organ development and maturation are much more advanced by 70 days than described.
- The stages in the Hadith align with the ancient Greek understanding of embryology but contradict modern scientific knowledge.

This shows that while ancient ideas about embryology influenced the teachings, they do not align with our current understanding of human development.

Hadith's Stages of Prenatal Development

1. **Stage 1:** Sperm – for 40 days
2. **Stage 2:** 'Alaqa – clot for 40 days
3. **Stage 3:** Mudagha – flesh for 40 days

This makes a total of 120 days, or 3 months, with no bones formed yet. However, modern studies show that at just two months, the organs are formed, bones are starting to calcify, and muscles are already moving.

This Hadith states that the fetus doesn't become "an unformed lump" until 80 days, which is a clear error. Dr. Maurice Bucaille also mentions this Hadith and concludes, "This description of embryonic evolution does not agree with modern data."

The Theological Problem

The scientific errors in this Hadith raise questions about the theological accuracy of the Hadiths. If this Hadith is scientifically incorrect, how can we be sure about the accuracy of other Hadiths that don't contain obvious scientific mistakes?

Furthermore, how do we know that the Hadith is not an accurate transmission of Muhammad's understanding? If the Qur'an says that human development starts from "a sperm-drop" which becomes a clot ('alaqa), does it accurately represent the scientific understanding of the time?

Modern interpretations of the word **'alaqa** claim it means "leech-like substance" as some contemporary Muslims, like Shabir Ally, suggest. However, earlier scholars of Greek medicine used the term **'alaqa** to explain the human development process. This leads to confusion regarding the correct interpretation.

Avicenna (Ibn Sina) on Embryology

Avicenna (980-1037 AD) wrote about human formation, referencing the role of the male sperm and the female menstrual blood:

- "The human being takes its origin from two things: (1) the male sperm, which plays the part of 'factor'; (2) the female sperm [menstrual blood], which provides the matter."
- He agrees with the Greek idea that the embryo begins as a clot, which fits with the Qur'an's description of creation from a "clot" (Qur'an 96:2).

Ibn Qayyim Al-Jawziyya (1291-1351 AD)

Ibn Qayyim's writing illustrates the connection between Greek medicine and the Qur'an. In his works, he explains how the Qur'an corresponds with the teachings of Hippocrates, Galen, and others:

- He references Hippocrates' idea that the semen grows because of the mother's blood.
- He also mentions the creation of the embryo through different stages, just as the Greek doctors described.

- Importantly, Ibn Qayyim did not challenge Greek medicine but showed the agreement between the Qur'an and these medical teachings.

Imam Naasir-addiin Baidawi's Commentary

Imam Baidawi, in his commentary (1282 AD), explains the word **'alaqa** as "a piece of solid blood" and **mudagha** as "a piece of meat as much as can be chewed." This aligns with the Greek understanding of human embryonic development.

Stages of Embryology – A Modern Idea?

It has been suggested that the Qur'an's depiction of embryology is a modern prophecy of embryology. However, we see that ancient medical knowledge, including the works of Hippocrates, Aristotle, and Galen, also divided embryonic development into stages.

Even after the Qur'an, Islamic scholars continued to teach these stages, and the descriptions remained consistent with the ideas of Galen and other ancient physicians.

For instance, modern embryologists like Dr. Keith Moore confirm that muscles and bones form simultaneously in the fetus, contrary to the Qur'an's order of bones forming first and then being covered with muscles. Furthermore, **'alaqa** in the Qur'an is best understood as "clot," which was the accepted meaning of the word at the time.

Conclusion

The stages of human development described in the Qur'an reflect the ancient Greek understanding of embryology, which we now know is scientifically incorrect. These ideas were widely accepted in Muhammad's time and were passed down in Islamic teachings. However, with modern scientific knowledge, we now understand that both the Qur'an and ancient Greek teachings on embryology are mistaken.

CHAPTER 4

Errors on Semen Production in the Quran

The Quran suggests that semen is produced in the area between the ribs and the back:

"Now let man think from what he is created! He is created from a drop emitted - proceeding from between the backbone and the ribs." (Sura 86:5-7)

Dr. William Campbell explains why this verse is inconsistent with modern medical understanding: The verse mentions that man is created from a "gushing fluid" that comes from the area between the "loins" and "ribs" (sometimes translated as "backbone" instead of "loins"). This suggests that semen comes from a physical place in the body, namely between the back or kidney area, instead of from the testicles.

Since this verse refers to the moment of reproduction, it can't be describing embryonic development. The terms "sulb" (meaning back or loins) and "tara'ib" (referring to the ribs or chest) point to a physical process, and not a metaphor. This leaves us with the issue that the Quran mistakenly places semen production in the back or kidney area, rather than the testicles.

Dr. Bucaille, a physician, acknowledges this issue and, in discussing the verse, admits that the translation may be more of an interpretation than an accurate rendering of the original text. He finds the verse "hardly comprehensible," especially in the context of modern science.

Translations of Sura 86:5-7

Here are various translations of the verse:

- **Abdullah Yusuf Ali** (Egyptian, 1946): "He is created from a drop emitted—proceeding from between the backbone and the ribs."
- **Muhammad Marmaduke Pickthall** (English, 1977): "He is created from a gushing fluid that issued from between the loins and ribs."
- **Muhammad Zafrulla Khan** (Pakistani, 1971): "He is created from a fluid poured forth, which issues forth from between the loins and the breastbones."
- **Muhammad Hamidullah** (French, 1981): "Il a été créé d'une giclée d'eau sortie d'entre lombes et côtes" ("He was created from a spurt of water coming out between the loins and ribs").
- **D. Masson** (French, 1967): "Il a été créé d'une goutte d'eau répandue sortie d'entre les lombes et les côtes" ("He was created from a drop of spread-out water coming out between the loins and the ribs").

These translations all align closely, reflecting the original text's description of semen being emitted from the area between the back and the ribs.

Dr. Bucaille's Interpretation

Dr. Bucaille suggests a different interpretation: he believes the verse should be understood as referring to the sexual organs of both men and women. He proposes that the word **sulb** refers to the male sexual area, while **tara'ib** refers to the female sexual area. According to his explanation, the fluid comes from the "conjunction" of these areas, which he argues aligns better with modern scientific understanding.

However, when compared with the translations above, Dr. Bucaille's interpretation is not a direct translation of the original Arabic. His explanation relies on assumptions:

1. **Sulb** does not traditionally refer to the male sexual area in the 1st-century Arabic usage.
2. The phrase "as a result of the conjunction" cannot be derived from the words **min bain**, which literally means "from between."
3. **Tara'ib** is only used once in the Quran and is more commonly understood as referring to the chest or ribs, not the female sexual area.

No dictionaries support the idea that **tara'ib** refers to the female genital area. Dr. Bucaille has not provided any examples from historical Arabic literature to support this interpretation, which raises questions about the validity of his explanation.

Conclusion

In conclusion, the Quran's description of semen production in Sura 86:5-7 conflicts with modern medical knowledge, and no valid linguistic evidence supports the interpretation that **tara'ib** refers to the female genitalia. Dr. Bucaille's attempt to reinterpret the verse does not hold up under scrutiny, and the traditional translations that link the verse to the back and kidney area remain consistent with the text's original meaning.

The Quran on Semen Production

Some Muslims argue that the Quran isn't referring to the production of semen itself, but to the area that supplies the testes with the necessary blood for semen production. A typical response, such as the one presented by the Learner, suggests:

The latter part of Sura 86:5-7, which mentions "emanating from a place between the (lower) back and the (lower) ribs," has been interpreted by some as referring to the region between these points in the abdomen. After consulting with medical professionals, the Learner was told that while semen is produced in the testes, the blood supply essential for its production comes from the area between the ribs and back. Based on this, the Learner argues that the Quranic verse could be referring to the initial emanation of semen, rather than its final form, which would make the verse scientifically accurate.

However, there are problems with this interpretation. Dr. Jamal Badawi and Dr. Zakir Naik, two prominent Islamic scholars, have made similar claims in their works. They argue that the verse refers to the region that supplies the blood for semen production, not the semen itself.

The Issue with this Interpretation

The problem with the above explanation is that both Dr. Naik, Dr. Badawi, and the Learner are Sunni Muslims. As stated on the Learner's website, they base their understanding of Islam solely on the Quran and the Sunnah of the Prophet Muhammad. This means that rather than interpreting the Quran through modern scientific understanding, they must turn to the traditional interpretations given by Muhammad and his followers.

However, when we refer to these early interpretations, we find that Muhammad and his followers understood Sura 86:5-7 in a way that contradicts modern scientific knowledge about human anatomy. According to the commentary from **Tafsir Ibn Kathir**:

"He is created from a water gushing forth. "This refers to the sexual fluid coming from both the man and the woman. The passage continues: "Proceeding from between the backbone and the ribs," which means the backbone of the man and the ribs of the woman. Ibn Kathir further explains that the fluid from both the man and the woman contributes to the creation of the child.

Early Muslim Understanding

According to Ibn Kathir, the first Muslims believed that the child was created from the sexual fluid of both the man and the woman. This suggests that early Islamic teachings held the view that women contributed sperm, which determined the child's characteristics, including gender.

Hadiths on Semen and Child Characteristics

Additional hadiths support the idea that both the male and female contribute to the child's characteristics. For instance, Muhammad is quoted as saying:

"As for the resemblance of the child to its parents; if a man has sexual intercourse with his wife and gets a discharge first, the child will resemble the father, and if the woman gets her discharge first, the child will resemble her." (Sahih al-Bukhari, Volume 4, Number 546)

In another hadith:

"Does a woman get a (nocturnal sexual) discharge?" asked Um Salama. Muhammad responded, "How then does her son resemble her?" (Sahih al-Bukhari, Volume 8, Book 73, Number 113)

These teachings reflect the belief that the characteristics and gender of a child were influenced by both the male and female sexual fluids.

Conclusion

In conclusion, while modern Muslim scholars may attempt to reconcile the Quran's description of semen production with contemporary medical knowledge, the traditional understanding rooted in early Islamic teachings is quite different. Both the Quran and hadiths imply that the male and female sexual fluids both play a role in determining a child's characteristics, including gender. However, this understanding is in conflict with modern scientific knowledge of human reproduction.

The Quran and the Role of Female Sperm

A hadith clarifies that Muhammad spoke of the female contribution to reproduction, specifically referring to female sperm. The hadith narrates an interaction where the Prophet explains the formation of a child based on the dominance of the male or female fluid:

"The reproductive substance of man is white and that of woman yellow. When the male's substance prevails upon the female's, a male child is formed, and when the female's substance prevails, a female child is formed." (Sahih Muslim)

This idea aligns with ancient Greek thought, particularly the beliefs of Hippocrates, who claimed that both men and women contribute sperm, and the gender of the child is determined by which sperm is stronger or more abundant.

Historical Context: Greek Influence on Muhammad's Understanding

The notion that both men and women produce sperm comes from Greek medical theories. Hippocrates believed that both genders contributed sperm, and the child's gender depended on which sperm overpowered the other. This idea is echoed in the Quran and hadiths, where the male and female fluids are said to determine the child's sex.

Dr. Lactantius also notes that the Quran's references to sperm and the reproductive fluids align with the understanding of Greek physicians. These ancient beliefs, which lacked modern scientific insight, suggest that Muhammad's understanding of human reproduction may have been influenced by Greek medical theories, especially since both sperm and menstrual blood were believed to contribute to the formation of the child.

Alternate Interpretations of Quranic Verses

Some Muslims propose that the Quran's reference to "the back and the ribs" in Sura 86:5-7 is a euphemism for the male sexual organ. The Learner, a Muslim scholar, argues that the Quran avoids direct mention of the male sexual organ and uses euphemistic language instead. He suggests that the reference to the "back and the ribs" was meant to convey the source of semen, while maintaining the Quran's literary value.

While this interpretation attempts to reconcile the text with modern sensibilities, it does not address the scientific inaccuracies in the Quranic description of semen production, which contradicts what we now understand about human anatomy and reproduction.

The Problem with Modern Interpretations

The major issue with these interpretations is that they rely on modern explanations that retroactively apply contemporary understanding to the Quran. However, the original Arabic text, as understood by Muhammad and his early followers, aligns more closely with the outdated Greek theories on reproduction.

Dr. Bucaille's attempt to reinterpret the Quran's reference to the male and female fluids, along with the Learner's euphemistic approach, fails to resolve the contradictions between the Quranic account and modern scientific knowledge. Instead of presenting accurate medical knowledge, the Quran appears to reflect the ancient, scientifically incorrect views held by Greek physicians.

Conclusion

In conclusion, the Quran's teachings on reproduction, including the role of female sperm, are rooted in the outdated theories of ancient Greek physicians. The hadiths further reinforce the idea that both the male and female contribute to the child's formation, an idea that was widely accepted in pre-modern times but has since been disproven by modern science. While modern Muslim scholars may attempt to reinterpret these verses, the historical and scientific context reveals that the Quran's descriptions of reproduction are inconsistent with modern medical knowledge.

In the following hadith, it becomes clear that Muhammad was speaking about the actual female reproductive system when he referred to female sperm:

Hadith Reference:

Thauban, the freed slave of Muhammad (peace be upon him), narrated that a Jewish rabbi came to Muhammad and asked him various questions. When the subject of conception came up, the Prophet stated:

"The reproductive substance of man is white and that of woman yellow. When the male's substance prevails upon the female's substance, a male child is created by Allah's decree, and when the female's substance prevails upon the male's substance, a female child is formed by the decree of Allah." (Sahih Muslim)

This statement aligns with the ancient Greek belief that both men and women contribute sperm, and that the gender of the child depends on which sperm—male or female—prevails. In this case, Muhammad's view echoes the Greek understanding of reproduction, where both sexes were believed to contribute equally to the child's creation.

The Influence of Greek Medical Theories

This view of female sperm is not unique to Muhammad but reflects the medical theories of ancient Greece. Dr. Lactantius explains that in the Quran, the term "nutfah" (translated as "drop of sperm") refers to the male sperm, while the "yellow fluid" from the female corresponds to the concept of female sperm. This is an idea derived from Greek medicine, where both male and female fluids were thought to contribute to conception, even though they had no knowledge of sperm cells or eggs as we understand them today.

Dr. Moore, a medical expert, attempts to translate "nutfah" as "mingled fluid," which he interprets as the fluids from both male and female containing their respective gametes. However, the Quran does not explicitly mention sperm or eggs. Instead, it uses the word "nutfah," which can be translated as semen or, at most, "germinal fluid"—a term used by the Greeks like Hippocrates, who described male and female reproductive fluids.

The Hadith and the Interpretation of Female Sperm

Another hadith confirms the belief that both male and female contributed to the child's creation. It says:

"If a male's fluid prevails upon the female's substance, the child will be a male by Allah's decree, and when the substance of the female prevails, a female child is formed." (Sahih Muslim)

This is not an accurate reflection of modern genetics, where the sex of the child is determined by the male sperm carrying either an X or Y chromosome. Instead, this statement follows the ancient Greek belief that the male's and female's reproductive fluids determined the gender, based on which fluid prevailed in the process.

The hadith further clarifies that Muhammad believed the reproductive substance of men was "white," and that of women was "yellow," which parallels the ancient Greek concept. This terminology resembles descriptions found in the developing eggs of chickens, which were dissected by Aristotle.

Alternate Interpretations

Some scholars propose an alternative interpretation of the verse in Surah 86:5-7. The Learner, for instance, suggests that the phrase "between the ribs and the back" is a euphemism for the male sexual organ. He argues that the Quran avoids explicitly mentioning the male reproductive organ, and instead uses euphemistic language to refer to the source of sperm. However, this interpretation does not address the underlying issue of the Quran's scientific inaccuracies regarding reproduction.

Conclusion

In conclusion, the Quranic references to female sperm and the process of conception reflect ancient Greek medical theories, which lacked the scientific understanding we have today. Muhammad's statements about reproduction were based on the medical knowledge of his time, which included incorrect beliefs about the role of both male and female fluids in determining the gender and characteristics of the child. These ideas were not unique to Muhammad but were common among ancient physicians like Hippocrates and Aristotle.

Muhammad Asad also acknowledged that the term *farjahaa* literally refers to a woman's sexual organ. In his commentary on Surah 21:91, Asad writes:

"... As for the description of Mary as *allati ahsanat farjaha*, idiomatically denoting 'one who guarded her chastity' (lit., 'HER PRIVATE PARTS')..." (Asad, *The Message of the Qur'an* [Dar Al-Andalus Limited, 3 Library Ramp, Gibraltar, rpt. 1993], p. 500, f. 87; bold emphasis ours).

Here's another example that shows *farj* refers explicitly to the female genitalia:

Narrated Basrah: A man from the Ansar, called Basrah, said: "I married a virgin woman in her veil. When I entered upon her, I found her pregnant. I mentioned this to the Prophet (peace be upon him). The

Prophet said: 'She will receive her dower, for you made her VAGINA (*farj*) lawful for you. The child will be your slave. When she has borne (a child), flog her (according to the version of al-Hasan).'" (Sunan of Abu Dawud, Book 11, Number 2126)

Christian writer Abd al-Masih offers his perspective on the issue. Commenting on Surah 21:91, he writes:

"Whoever reads verse 91 of Surah al-Anbiya' 21 carefully could be embarrassed. It is scandalous how Muhammad and his spirit of revelation elevate Mary as the most important of all women, and at the same time, tear away her veil of chastity. Her self-protection is not described euphemistically, but brutally, as in a business transaction: 'And she guarded her vagina (*farj*), so We breathed into her of Our Spirit.' (Surah al-Anbiya' 21:91) This revelation is not an honor, but an exposure. Perhaps it was customary among Bedouins to speak contemptuously about women, but this only shows the rule of Arabic men and their contempt for women. If the best of women is spoken about like this, what about others? Men are never written about like this; they remain covered, holier-than-thou, and self-righteous." (Abd al-Masih, *Who Is The Spirit From Allah In Islam?* [Light of Life, P.O. Box 13, A-9503, VILLACH AUSTRIA], pp. 46-47)

The author continues to analyze Surah 66:12:

"The second problem is caused by the Arabic language. In Arabic, Allah does not say: 'so We breathed into her of Our Spirit,' but 'into him.' Who is it into whom the spirit was breathed? The embryo *'Isa?* That is difficult to accept, for then 'Isa would have existed in Mary's womb already before the spirit was breathed into her. That would mean Allah created 'Isa beforehand, or that he existed before he was conceived. Both options are out of the question for Islamic scholars. Who is it then, into whom the Spirit from Allah was breathed? IT IS ALMOST UNSPEAKABLE, but the last expression in the previous sentence, which is masculine in Arabic, IS THE EXPRESSION FOR MARY'S GENITALS. The literal meaning of Allah's statement in Arabic is then, 'So We breathed into her vagina (*farj*) of Our spirit.' This turns the stomachs of some of our readers."

Rudi Paret, a renowned Qur'anic translator into German, confirms the meaning of this phrase in a footnote, suggesting that many Islamic scholars find it blasphemous. Ibn Mas'ud even suggested that the Qur'anic text should be altered to avoid such uncomfortable interpretations.

Other References to a Woman's Sexual Area in the Quran

Another rather explicit reference to a woman's sexual area is found in:

"Surely, for the godfearing awaits a place of security, gardens and vineyards, and maidens of SWELLING BREASTS (*kawa'ib*), of like age, and a cup overflowing." (Surah 78:33, Arberry; see also Dawood, Rodwell)

Ibn Kathir comments on the meaning of *kawa'ib*:

"And vineyards, and *Kawa'ib Atrab,* meaning, wide-eyed maidens WITH FULLY DEVELOPED BREASTS. Ibn 'Abbas, Mujahid, and others have said, *Kawa'ib* means ROUND BREASTS. They meant that the breasts of these girls will be fully rounded and not sagging because they will be virgins, equal in age…" (Tafsir Ibn Kathir, Abridged, Volume 10, pp. 333-334; bold emphasis ours)

Similarly, ar-Razi stated:

"The *kawaib* are the buxom girls (*nawahid*) whose breasts have become FULL (*takaabat*) and ROUND (*tafallakat*)." (Tafsir ar-Razi, Volume 8, p. 311; bold emphasis ours).

These references are explicit and reflect the understanding of *farj* as referring to a woman's sexual organs in classical Islamic commentary.

Some Muslim scholars have acknowledged that certain Quranic descriptions can be quite graphic and even cause arousal in readers. For instance, G.F. Haddad addresses the issue of men having multiple wives in Paradise while women have only one husband, explaining:

"We do not know with certainty that there will be such a restriction on women, even though the reverse would hardly be mentionable to a decent woman. A woman in the traditional world would consider it horrible to be told, 'You can have all the men you want!' The Qur'an would never use inappropriate language. However, the Qur'an does say that in Paradise—both male and female inhabitants—'There wait on them immortal youths' (56:17), 'There serve them youths of everlasting youth, whom, when you see them, you would take for scattered pearls' (76:19). If this doesn't make a believing woman happy, then, as Imam al-Shafi'i said to one who is not moved by erotic poetry, 'You have no feelings.'" (Haddad, *Sex with Slaves and Women's Rights*; Source: MAC.ABC.SE)

The term *ghusl* refers to the ritual purification that a Muslim must undergo after sexual relations or a seminal discharge. Haddad is suggesting that Surah 78:33 may arouse a person so much that they could even experience a sexual release upon hearing it.

The concept of sexual relations in Paradise has led some Muslims to interpret these verses metaphorically. They argue that the descriptions are simply poetic attempts to express the indescribable.

However, such interpretations are problematic, as Muhammad himself did not allow for metaphorical readings. In Sahih Muslim, no. 6793 and 6797, it is stated:

"In Paradise... every person would have two wives (so beautiful) that the marrow of their shanks would glimmer beneath the flesh, and there would be none without a wife in Paradise."

Further, in *Mishkat Al-Masabih*, Muhammad is quoted as saying:

"The believer will be given such and such strength in Paradise for sexual intercourse. It was questioned: O prophet of Allah! Can he do that? He said: 'He will be given the strength of one hundred persons.'" (Bk. IV, chp. XLII, Hadith no. 24; transmitted by Tirmizi)

Bilal Philips addresses the symbolic interpretations of these verses:

"Some translators of the Qur'an, trying to appeal to a Western audience, have wrongly interpreted the clear references to sexual pleasure in Paradise as symbolic. For instance, in his commentary on Surah 2:25, Abdullah Yusuf Ali states that the reference to 'pure' wives in Paradise negates any physical associations of sex. However, this interpretation contradicts many Quranic verses and Prophetic traditions that clearly discuss the physical aspects of Paradise. The term 'Mutahharatun' (pure) actually refers to bodies in Paradise being free of decay, such as the wine, honey, and milk of Paradise, which are not intoxicating or sour. Therefore, Yusuf Ali's attempt to spiritualize these verses misrepresents the clear physical reality described in the Qur'an." (Bilal Philips, *Ibn Taymeeyah's Essay on the Jinn (Demons)*, 1998, pp. 28-30)

This highlights that some of the earlier interpretations of the Qur'an's references to Paradise may be misunderstood or misrepresented when trying to fit them into modern cultural perspectives. The imagery in these verses, particularly surrounding sexual pleasure in Paradise, is much more explicit in its original context.

Even more striking is Ibn Kathir's commentary on Surah 56:35-37:

Abu Dawud At-Tayalisi recorded that Anas reported that the Messenger of Allah said: "In Paradise, the believer will be given such strength for women." Anas asked, "O Allah's Messenger, will one be able to do that?" He replied, "He will be given the strength of a hundred (men)." At-Tirmidhi also recorded this and classified it as "Sahih Gharib." Abu Al-Qasim At-Tabarani recorded that Abu Hurayrah said the Messenger of Allah was asked, "O Allah's Messenger, will we have sexual intercourse with our wives in Paradise?" He answered: "The man will be able to have sexual intercourse with a hundred virgins in one day." Al-Hafiz Abu Abdullah Al-Maqisi stated, "In my view, this Hadith meets the criteria of Sahih, and Allah knows best." (Tafsir Ibn Kathir - Abridged, Volume 9, Surat Al-Jathiyah to the end of Surat Al-Munafiqun, pp. 429-430)

Given these examples, the explanation offered by the Learner seems flawed. Both the Quran and Islamic traditions clearly describe women's sexual organs, often in explicit detail. Therefore, according to the Learner's own reasoning, the Quran cannot be considered decent literature due to its graphic depiction of women's sexual anatomy, the claim that Allah breathed into a woman's sexual organ for conception, or the descriptions of virgins in paradise having firm, round breasts. The language of the Quran in reporting the conception of Jesus is undeniably crude and inappropriate.

Moreover, the description of the maidens in paradise is not a neutral, factual statement (such as "these maidens will be perfect in every regard"). Instead, it is designed to stimulate sexual desire and entice listeners to strive for paradise, a place where these maidens await the faithful. This approach is similar to how modern advertisers use sexually suggestive imagery of women to sell products, such as cars. Therefore, the Quran is using a direct appeal to men's sexual desires to encourage belief in and support for Islam.

In light of these points, we conclude that the Learner's explanation seems more like an attempt to protect the Quran from scientific errors than a proper interpretation of the text. The interpretation of Surah 86:5-7 proposed by Dr. Badawi, Dr. Naik, and the Learner is more of a personal interpretation that seeks to align the Quran with modern scientific understanding. To do so, they must ignore the authentic interpretations of the Prophet and his companions, which leads to conflicts with both the Quran and Hadith. As a result, science, not the Quran, has become the standard by which God's "revelation" is critiqued.

It is worth noting that the Learner does acknowledge that the Quran is not a scientific textbook and that the verses in question should be understood within their historical context. The Learner claims that these verses had significance to the people who first heard the Quran in the seventh century, and that modern scientific knowledge should not dictate their interpretation. However, even with this approach, we find that the early Muslim understanding of Surah 86:5-7 does not align with modern scientific knowledge.

CHAPTER 5

The Quran presents a View of the Earth that suggest it is Flat

The Structure of the Universe: Quranic Views on Earth and Heaven

Contradictions About the Shape of the Earth

The Quran presents a view of the earth that suggests it is flat, with mountains as pegs to keep it stable. It also describes the heavens as a roof or dome covering the earth. Additionally, the Quran implies that the earth is stationary, not moving. In this section, we will refer to various Quranic verses and, when needed, the interpretations of the famous Muslim scholar Ibn Kathir. We will mostly use the English edition of Ibn Kathir's Tafsir, translated under the supervision of

Shaykh Safiur Rahman Al-Mubarakpuri, which is available online at
www.tafsir.com.

Quran 2:22

"Who made the earth a bed for you, and the heaven a roof, and caused
water to come down from the clouds and brought forth fruits for your
sustenance; so do not set up equals to Allah, while you know." - Sher
Ali

Commentary:
The verse explains that Allah made the earth flat, like a bed, and placed
mountains on it to stabilize it. It also states that the heavens are a roof
covering the earth. (Tafsir Ibn Kathir, Part 1, Surah Al-Fatihah and
Surah Al-Baqarah, pp. 79-80)

Online version:

The earth is made a resting place, just like a bed, stabilized with firm
mountains, and the sky is described as a canopy or ceiling. (Source:
tafsir.com)

Quran 13:3

"And He it is who hath outstretched the earth, and placed on it firm
mountains, and rivers; and of every fruit He hath placed on it two
kinds; He causeth the night to enshroud the day. Verily in this are signs
for those who reflect." - Rodwell

Commentary:
Allah, in His power and authority, raised the heavens without visible
pillars, making them distant and above the earth. The first heaven is
five hundred years away from the earth, with a thickness of five
hundred years, and the same applies to the other heavens. It's

explained that the heaven is like a dome over the earth, without visible pillars. (Source: tafsir.com)

Quran 15:19

"And the earth have We spread out, and set therein firm mountains and cause everything to grow therein in proper proportion." - Sher Ali

Commentary:
The earth is spread out flat, with firm mountains placed to prevent it from swaying and to keep everything in balance. (Source: altafsir.com)

Quran 16:15

"And He has set up on the earth mountains standing firm, lest it should shake with you; and rivers and roads; that ye may guide yourselves." - Y. Ali

Commentary:
Mountains are placed on the earth to keep it stable, preventing it from shaking, so creatures can live safely. (Source: tafsir.com)

Quran 20:53

"[Since He is the One] Who has laid out the earth as a carpet for you and has traced highways on it for you, and sent down water from the sky, We have brought forth every sort of plant with it, of various types." - T.B. Irving

Quran 22:65

"Do you not see that Allah has made subservient to you whatsoever is in the earth and the ships running in the sea by His command? And He withholds the heaven from falling on the earth except with His permission; most surely Allah is Compassionate, Merciful to men." - Shakir

In these verses, the Quran's portrayal of the earth as flat, stable, and covered by a fixed dome-like heaven is at odds with modern scientific understanding of the earth's spherical shape and dynamic atmosphere.

Commentary:
"He withholds the heaven from falling on the earth except by His leave" implies that if Allah willed, He could allow the sky to fall onto the earth, causing destruction and death. However, by His mercy and power, He prevents the sky from falling, unless He chooses to allow it. (Source: tafsir.com)

Note: While it is true that God, as the Creator, has set everything in place and continues to sustain the world, this idea that the sky is heavy and could fall is scientifically inaccurate. The sky is not a solid, heavy object that could cause harm if it fell, making this view contradictory to modern science.

Quran 27:61

"Is not He (better than your gods) Who has made the earth as a fixed abode, and has placed rivers in its midst, and has placed firm mountains therein, and has set a barrier between the two seas (of salt and sweet water). Is there any ilah (god) with Allah? Nay, but most of them know not." - Hilali-Khan

Alternative Translations:

- "Is not He (best) Who made the earth a fixed abode..." - Pickthall
- "He who made the earth a fixed place..." - A.J. Arberry

Commentary:

The verse suggests that the earth is stable and stationary, meaning it does not move or shake. If the earth were to shift or convulse, it would not be a livable place. By Allah's grace, the earth remains calm and unshaken. (Source: tafsir.com)

Quran 30:25

"Among His signs are [the fact] that the sky and earth hold firm at His command. Then whenever He calls you forth out of the earth once and for all, you will (all) come forth!" - Irving

Commentary:

This verse highlights the power of Allah to maintain the stability of the heavens and the earth. It is similar to verses about Allah holding the heavens and earth in place (22:65, 35:41). On the Day of Resurrection, Allah will bring forth the dead from their graves by His command. (Source: tafsir.com)

Quran 31:10

"He created the heavens without any pillars that ye can see; He set on the earth mountains standing firm, lest it should shake with you; and He scattered through it beasts of all kinds. We send down rain from the sky, and produce on the earth every kind of noble creature, in pairs." - Pickthall

Commentary:

The mountains are described as stabilizers for the earth, preventing it from shaking. This reference does not concern earthquakes as often claimed by some Muslims but suggests that the mountains provide stability to the earth. (Source: tafsir.com)

Quran 35:41

"Verily! Allah grasps the heavens and the earth lest they move away from their places, and if they were to move away from their places, there is not one that could grasp them after Him. Truly, He is Ever Most Forbearing, Oft Forgiving." - Hilali-Khan

Commentary:
The verse emphasizes that Allah holds the heavens and the earth in place, preventing them from moving from their positions. If they were to shift, no one else could keep them in place. (Source: tafsir.com)

One Muslim website openly admits that, according to the Quran, the heavens and earth are stationary.

Question:
ASSALAM-O-ALAIKUM, WHAT DOES SHARIA SAY ABOUT THE MOVEMENT OF THE EARTH? PLEASE EXPLAIN.

Answer:
According to the Quran and Hadith, the earth is stationary, and the sun and planets move. The Quran states that the sun moves around the earth, but the earth does not move around the sun. Several verses in the Quran discuss the movement of the sun and moon, like the following:

1. "And He made the sun and the moon subservient, each running to a fixed turn." (Al-Quran, Sura Al-Ra'ad 13:2)
2. "And He made the sun and the moon subservient to you, both constantly moving." (Al-Quran, Sura Ibraheem 14:23)

3. "Each of them (the moon and the sun) is floating in an orbit."
    (Al-Quran, Sura Yaseen 36:40)

It is clear from these verses that the sun moves, and Muslims are obligated to believe this as it is what Allah has revealed. The Quran also rejects the theory of the earth's rotation, stating: "Undoubtedly, Allah has withheld the heavens and the earth lest they move." (Al-Quran)

In the book *Fiq-hus-Sahaba Baad-Al-Khulfa-e-Alarba*, a statement by K'ab was recorded in front of Syedna Abdullah bin Masood and Syedna Huzaifa bin Alyaman. K'ab claimed, "The heaven revolves," but both Syedna Abdullah bin Masood and Syedna Huzaifa disagreed, stating that Allah has made the heavens and earth stationary. This view is confirmed by the companions of the Prophet (pbuh).

(Source: Bismikaallahuma.org by Prince ZED; bold emphasis ours)

Quranic Verses:

Q. 40:64

"It is God who made for you the earth a fixed place and heaven for an edifice; and He shaped you, and shaped you well, and provided you with the good things. That then is God, your Lord, so blessed be God, the Lord of all Being." - Arberry

Commentary:
"He made the earth stable and spread out so you can live on it and travel. He strengthened it with mountains to prevent it from shaking." (Source: tafsir.com)

Q. 43:10

"Who has made for you the earth like a carpet spread out, and has made for you roads (and channels) therein, in order that ye may find guidance (on the way)." - Y. Ali

Commentary:
"He made the earth smooth, stable, and firm so that you can travel and live on it without it shaking." (Source: tafsir.com)

Q. 50:6-7

"What, have they not beheld heaven above them, how We have built it, and decked it out fair, and it has no cracks? And the earth -- We stretched it forth, and cast on it firm mountains, and We caused to grow therein of every joyous kind." - Arberry

Commentary:
The heavens were created without any cracks, implying they are a solid structure. (Source: tafsir.com)

Q. 51:48

"And the earth We have spread out, and how excellently do We spread it out!" - Sher Ali

Q. 55:10

"It is He Who has spread out the earth for His creatures." - Pickthall

Q. 67:3-5

"Who hath created seven heavens in harmony. Thou (Muhammad) canst see no fault in the Beneficent One's creation; then look again: Canst thou see any rifts? Then look again and yet again, thy sight will return unto thee weakened and made dim. And verily We have beautified the world's heaven with lamps, and We have made them missiles for the devils, and for them We have prepared the doom of flame."

Conclusion:

The Quran teaches that the earth is stationary and does not move, as stated in various verses. These interpretations align with the traditional understanding of the earth in Islamic teachings.

Commentary:

Who could believe that stars or meteors, referred to as "lamps" in the Quran, are used as missiles against spiritual beings like devils? The verse, "Then look again. Can you see any rifts?" asks us to observe the sky closely, to see if there are any flaws or cracks in it. Ibn `Abbas, Mujahid, Ad-Dahhak, and others explain that this refers to visible "cracks" or "tears" in the sky. (Source: tafsir.com)

Q. 71:15-20

"Have you not considered how God created seven heavens, one upon another, and set the moon therein for a light, and the sun for a lamp? And God caused you to grow out of the earth, then He shall return you to it, and bring you forth. And God has laid the earth for you as a carpet, that you may tread its paths and ravines." - Arberry

The description of the heavens being stacked one on top of the other suggests that the author of the Quran mistakenly thought of the heavens as solid physical objects, similar to a dome. This would explain the mention of cracks in the heavens, as if they were something tangible. Ibn Kathir, in his commentary on Surah 2:29, uses a building analogy, saying that Allah first created the earth, then created the heavens as a multi-layered structure, just like constructing a building with multiple floors. (Source: tafsir.com)

Ibn Kathir's commentary on Q. 71:15-20:

"Allah has created the seven heavens in tiers and made the moon a light therein, and the sun a lamp" means that Allah created the sun and moon with distinct qualities, with the sun providing light for the day and the moon lighting the night. The moon's light changes throughout the month, as it waxes and wanes, marking the passage of time. (Source: tafsir.com)

Q. 78:6-7

"Have We not made the earth as a bed, and the mountains as pegs?" - Sher Ali

Commentary:
This verse describes the earth as a stable, peaceful resting place, firm and subservient to human life. The mountains are referred to as pegs, keeping the earth stable and preventing it from shaking. (Source: tafsir.com)

Q. 79:27-30

"What, are you stronger in constitution or the heaven He built? He lifted up its vault, leveled it, darkened its night, and brought forth its forenoon; and the earth – after that He spread it out." - Arberry

Commentary by Jalalayn:

The earth was created before the heavens, but it was not spread out until after the creation of the heavens. Allah then made it flat, so it could be a firm resting place for human beings. (Source: tafsir.com)

Q. 88:20

"And the earth, how it has been flattened out?" - Irving
"The earth, how it was made flat?" - N.J. Dawood

Commentary:

This verse asks the reader to reflect on how the mountains have been firmly set in place so that the earth does not shake. Allah made the mountains to be steady, and He created the earth smooth and spread out for humans to live on. The verse directs the Bedouin to think about the world around him: his camel, the sky above, the mountains in front of him, and the earth beneath. All of these things are proof of Allah's power and creativity. They should help him recognize that Allah is the Creator and Lord of everything and the only one deserving of worship.

The two Jalals' interpretation:

The earth is described as being "laid out flat," which suggests that the earth is flat, according to the opinion of many Islamic scholars. This contrasts with the view held by astronomers, who believe the earth is spherical. Although this view of the earth's flatness doesn't contradict the core principles of Islamic law, it reflects the belief of most scholars from the time of the Quran's revelation. (Tafsir al-Jalalayn)

Q. 91:5-6

"By the heaven and that which built it, and by the earth and that which extended it!" - Arberry

Commentary:

This verse speaks about how Allah created and spread out the earth. Several interpretations of "Tahaha" suggest that it means Allah made the earth spread out, or He gave it its proportions and features. Scholars like Mujahid, Qatadah, and Ibn Abbas agree on this interpretation.

Tafsir al-Jalalayn says that "Tahaha" refers to the earth being spread out, or laid out flat.

From these verses, it's clear that the Quran describes the earth as flat and stationary, held in place by mountains. It further mistakenly describes the sun and moon as traveling through the sky, while the earth remains fixed and motionless. These interpretations are supported by early Muslim scholars such as Ibn Kathir, whose views align with this reading of the Quran.

Islamic Cosmology in Light of Early Muslim Exegesis of Surah 68:1

We will now provide interpretations from Islamic scholars and Muslim traditions that show a belief in a flat and motionless earth. These interpretations focus on the letter "Nun" from Surah 68:1: "Nun. By the Pen and by the (Record) which (men) write."

We previously quoted Ibn Kathir extensively, so we will continue with his explanations here. Ibn Kathir provides traditions that offer insight into early Muslim views of the cosmos. Some of these traditions may be surprising, especially for Muslims who may not be aware of them. It is worth noting that these traditions are included in the Arabic version of Ibn Kathir's Commentary but are omitted from the English translation.

We won't be quoting all of the traditions, but we will focus on those that are relevant to early Muslim views about the earth and the universe. We are grateful to our friend Dimitrius for translating these texts from Arabic, which allows us to share them with English-speaking readers.

According to early Islamic traditions, "Nun" refers to a great whale that swims in the waters of the vast ocean. This whale carries the seven earths on its back. Imam Abu Jafar Ibn Jarir shared this explanation based on narrations from Ibn Abbas.

1. **Creation of the Pen and the Nun**
   - The first thing Allah created was the Pen. Allah commanded the Pen, "Write." The Pen asked, "What should I write?" Allah replied, "Write everything that will happen from now until Judgment Day." The Pen then wrote the fate of all creation.
   - After this, Allah created the "Nun," the great whale. He caused steam to rise from the whale, which was used to form the heavens. Allah then laid the earth flat on the back of the whale.

2. **The Earth Stabilized by Mountains**
   - When the whale moved nervously, the earth began to shake. To stabilize the earth, Allah anchored it with mountains, ensuring it would remain firm and not sway.

3. **Additional Narrations**
   - Another narration, also from Ibn Abbas, states that Allah created the Nun above the waters and pressed the earth onto its back.
   - Al-Tabarani shared a similar hadith where the Prophet Muhammad (peace be upon him) explained that Allah first created the Pen and the whale. He instructed the Pen to write everything that would occur until the end of time. He then said, "Nun. By the Pen and by what they write," identifying the Nun as the whale and the Pen as "al-Qalam."

4. **Structure Beneath the Earth**
   - Some scholars, like Ibn Abu Nujaih, reported that the Nun is beneath the seven earths.
   - Al-Baghawy and others added more details: on the back of the whale is a massive rock, thicker than the width of the heavens and the earth. On top of this rock stands a bull with forty thousand horns. The seven

earths and everything within them are placed on the bull's body.

These descriptions reflect early cosmological interpretations within Islamic tradition. However, Allah knows best regarding the unseen realities of creation.

Al-Tabari's Explanation of Surah 68:1 with Citations

Renowned Muslim historian and exegete, Al-Tabari, offered detailed interpretations regarding the meaning of Surah 68:1, which states: "Nun. By the Pen and by what they write." These interpretations often align with similar explanations from other Islamic scholars like Ibn Kathir, highlighting early Islamic cosmology.

The Creation of the Pen and the Nun (Fish)

Al-Tabari narrates that the first creation of Allah was the Pen. This is supported by a hadith from Ibn Abbas, transmitted through Wasil b. 'Abd al-A'la al-Asadi, Muhammad b. Fudayl, and Al-A'mash. According to this narration:

1. Allah created the Pen and commanded it to write.
   o The Pen asked, "What shall I write?"
   o Allah replied, "Write what is predestined."
2. The Pen then wrote everything that would occur until the Day of Judgment.
   o After this, Allah lifted water vapor, which formed the heavens.
   o Allah then created the Nun, a great fish, and spread the earth upon its back.

This narration adds that when the fish moved, the earth shook. To stabilize it, Allah created mountains, anchoring the earth firmly (Al-Tabari, *Tafsir al-Tabari*).

Parallel Narrations on Creation

Al-Tabari documents various versions of this narrative from different chains of transmission:

1. **Transmission by Ibn al-Muthanna**
   - Ibn al-Muthanna reported through Ibn Abi 'Adi, Shu'bah, and Sulayman (Al-A'mash):
     - The Pen was created first and wrote everything predestined.
     - Allah then lifted water vapor, creating the heavens.
     - The earth was spread on the back of the Nun (the fish).
     - When the fish moved, the earth quaked, and Allah stabilized it with mountains.
     - The mountains were described as towering structures that held the earth in place.
2. **Transmission by Tamim b. al-Muntasir**
   - Tamim narrated through Ishaq b. Yusuf and Sharik b. 'Abdallah al-Nakha'i:
     - The heavens were created from the water vapor.
     - The earth was then laid on the back of the fish, which caused it to shake.
     - Allah anchored the earth with mountains to prevent further movement.
   - This version adds a slight variation where the heavens are described as being "split off" from the vapor.
3. **Transmission by Ibn Bashshar**
   - This narration, through Yahya, Sufyan, and Al-A'mash, reiterates the same sequence of events:
     - The Pen was created and instructed to write.
     - The heavens were formed from vapor, and the earth was spread on the fish's back.
     - The fish's agitation caused the earth to shake, leading Allah to create mountains to stabilize it.
4. **Transmission by Ibn Humayd**

- o In this narration, transmitted through Jarir b. 'Abd al-Hamid, 'Ata' b. al-Sa'ib, and Abu al-Duha Muslim b. Subayh:
  - Allah created the Pen, which wrote everything until the Day of Judgment.
  - Allah then created the fish and placed the earth upon its back.

Significance of "Nun" and the Cosmological Framework

Al-Tabari and other early commentators interpret "Nun" in Surah 68:1 as referring to this great fish. This cosmological framework, rooted in early Islamic tradition, portrays the universe as layered, with the earth resting on the fish, which itself is stabilized by mountains. Al-Tabari emphasizes that these traditions were considered sound by scholars such as Ibn Abbas and others (*Tafsir al-Tabari*).

References

- Al-Tabari, *Tafsir al-Tabari* (translated by Franz Rosenthal in *The History of Al-Tabari: General Introduction and From the Creation to the Flood*, State University of New York Press, 1989).
- Ibn Kathir, *Tafsir Ibn Kathir* (Abridged).
- Quranic commentary from *altafsir.com*.

These accounts reflect the early Islamic worldview and theological narratives concerning the creation of the universe.

Al-Tabari and the Creation Narrative: Commentary on Surah 68:1

Al-Tabari's Transmission

Renowned historian and exegete Al-Tabari recorded detailed accounts of the creation narrative based on early Islamic traditions. These traditions often explain Surah 68:1: "Nun. By the Pen and by what they write," with cosmological imagery, drawing connections between the Pen (al-Qalam), the whale (Nun), and the formation of the heavens and earth. Below are his interpretations and citations.

Creation of the Pen and the Nun (Whale)

According to Al-Tabari, the first creation was the Pen. This is based on the authority of Ibn 'Abbas, transmitted by Wasil b. 'Abd al-A'la al-Asadi, Muhammad b. Fudayl, and Al-A'mash:

1. **The Creation of the Pen**:
    - Allah created the Pen and commanded it to write.
    - The Pen asked, "What shall I write?"
    - Allah replied, "Write what is predestined."
    - The Pen wrote everything that would occur until the Day of Judgment.
2. **The Creation of the Heavens and Earth**:
    - Allah lifted water vapor, forming the heavens.
    - He created the whale (Nun) and spread the earth on its back.
    - The whale moved, causing the earth to shake. To stabilize it, Allah anchored the earth with mountains.
    - This is explained as: "Nun. By the Pen and what they write" (Surah 68:1).

Citations:

- *The History of Al-Tabari: General Introduction and From the Creation to the Flood*, translated by Franz Rosenthal (SUNY Press, 1989), Vol. 1, pp. 218-220.

Al-Tabari's Additional Descriptions

Al-Tabari provided supplementary details from various narrators:

1. **Narration by Ibn Bashshar:**

- o The heavens were formed from water vapor.
- o The earth was placed on the whale's back, which shook and caused quaking.
- o Mountains were created to stabilize the earth.

2. **Narration by Ibn Humayd**:
   - o Allah created the Pen to write everything until the Day of Judgment.
   - o He created the whale and placed the earth upon it.

Description of the "Haykal" (Cosmic Framework)

Al-Tabari further relayed a tradition narrated by Muhammad b. Sahl b. 'Askar:

- The heavens, earth, and oceans are encompassed by the "Haykal," a framework like ropes fastening a tent.
- The Haykal rests upon the Footstool (Kursi) of Allah.
- The earths are described as seven flat layers with oceans between them, all resting on the back of the whale (Nun).

Reference: *The History of Al-Tabari*, Vol. 1, pp. 207-208.

Al-Qurtubi's Commentary on Surah 68:1

The Pen and the Nun

Al-Qurtubi echoes Al-Tabari's interpretations, presenting additional details about the Pen and the whale. Narrated by Abu Hurayrah, the Prophet Muhammad stated:

1. **The Pen's Role**:
   - o Allah created the Pen first and commanded it to write all that will occur until the Day of Judgment.
2. **Creation of the Whale**:

- o Allah created the whale (Nun) above the waters.
- o The earth was pressed onto the whale's back and secured with mountains to prevent it from swaying.

Names of the Whale

Various names for the whale are provided:

- *Al-Bahmout* (Al-Kalbi and Mukatil).
- *Leotha* (Abu Yakthan and Al-Waqidi).
- *Lo-tho-tha* (Kab).

Kab narrated a story of Satan whispering to the whale to throw off the earth, but Allah sent a reptile to crawl into the whale's blowhole, stopping it from acting on Satan's suggestion.

Key Themes in Early Islamic Cosmology

1. **The Universe as a Structured Entity**:
   - o The heavens are layered, and the earth is flat, resting on a whale.
   - o Mountains function as stabilizers for the earth.
2. **Divine Control Over Creation**:
   - o Allah's direct involvement in controlling the cosmos is emphasized, from stabilizing the earth to stopping the whale from rebellion.

References:

- *The History of Al-Tabari*, Vol. 1, pp. 207-220.
- *Tafsir Al-Qurtubi*.
- Primary sources cited at quran.al-islam.com.

This narrative reflects early Islamic interpretations of cosmology, showcasing a blend of theological and mythical elements in understanding the universe.

Tafsir Ibn Abbas and Other Traditions on Creation

Tafsir Ibn Abbas on Surah 68:1 ("Nun")

And from his narration on the authority of Ibn 'Abbas that he said regarding the interpretation of Allah's saying (Nun): '(Nun) He says: Allah swears by the Nun, **which is the whale that carries the earths on its back while in Water, and beneath which is the Bull and under the Bull is the Rock and under the Rock is the Dust and none knows what is under the Dust save Allah**. The name of the whale is Liwash, and it is said its name is Lutiaya'; the name of the bull is Bahamut, and some say its name is Talhut or Liyona. The whale is in a sea called 'Adwad, and it is like a small bull in a huge sea. The sea is in a hollowed rock whereby there is 4,000 cracks, and from each crack water springs out to the earth. It is also said that Nun is one of the names of the Lord; it stands for the letter Nun in Allah's name al-Rahman (the Beneficent); and it is also said that a Nun is an inkwell. (By the pen) Allah swore by the pen. This pen is made of light and its height is equal to the distance between Heaven and earth. It is with this pen that the Wise Remembrance, i.e. the Guarded Tablet, was written. It is also said that the pen is one of the angels by whom Allah has sworn, (and that which they write (therewith)) and Allah also swore by what the angels write down of the works of the children of Adam, (*Tanwîr al-Miqbâs min Tafsîr Ibn 'Abbâs*; source al tafsir.com; bold and underline emphasis ours)

Ibn Abbas, one of the most prominent early Islamic scholars, provided detailed commentary on the meaning of "Nun" in Surah 68:1. According to his interpretation:

1. **"Nun" as a Whale**:
    o   Ibn Abbas states that "Nun" refers to a massive whale carrying the earths on its back while floating in water.

- o Beneath the whale lies a bull (*Bahamut* or *Talhut*), under which is a rock, followed by dust.
- o No one but Allah knows what lies beneath the dust.

2. **The Whale's Name**:
   - o The whale is referred to as *Liwash* or *Lutiaya*, while the bull has names like *Bahamut*, *Talhut*, or *Liyona*.
   - o The whale exists in a sea called 'Adwad, which is compared to a small bull in a vast ocean.

3. **The Pen and the Inkwell**:
   - o Allah created the Pen (*al-Qalam*), made of light, and commanded it to write all that will happen until Judgment Day.
   - o The Pen wrote everything on the Guarded Tablet (*al-Lawh al-Mahfuz*).

Source: *Tanwîr al-Miqbâs min Tafsîr Ibn 'Abbâs* (available at altafsir.com).

Other Interpretations and Hadiths

Mount Qaf and the Seven Earths

Several Muslim commentators and narrators provide additional cosmological descriptions, often intertwined with mythological elements:

1. **Mount Qaf**:
   - o The earth's stability is attributed to Mount Qaf, a massive range surrounding the earth. The veins of all mountains are connected to it.
   - o These mountains act as pegs, stabilizing the earth to prevent movement. (*Surah 21:31*)

2. **Seven Earths and Seas**:
   - o According to Al-Kisa'i, the earth is surrounded by seven seas, each enclosing the other. The last sea, *Baki*, encircles the entire creation.

- o Beneath the earth are seven layers, each inhabited by unique creatures, including nations punished for their sins and fantastical beings.

Creation of the Earth on a Whale

Kaab al-Ahbar narrates:

- Allah created dry land by commanding the wind to churn the waters. The foam from the waters solidified into land.
- The whale (*Nun*) carries the seven earths on its back, stabilized by mountains.

Source: *Qisas al-Anbiya* (Tales of the Prophets).

Other Hadiths on Creation

Hadith from Sunan Abu Dawud

The Prophet Muhammad described the structure of the heavens and the earth:

1. **Heavens and Oceans**:
   - o The distance between each heaven and the next is seventy years. Above the seventh heaven is a vast ocean, and above it are eight mountain goats.
   - o Allah's throne is above these layers.

Source: *Sunan Abu Dawud*, Book 40, Number 4705.

Hadith from Al-Tirmidhi

This narration links creation to divine power:

1. **Creation and Stability**:

- o When Allah created the earth, it oscillated. To stabilize it, mountains were created.
- o The angels marveled at the strength of the mountains, which Allah declared to be surpassed only by iron, fire, water, wind, and ultimately, human charity.

Source: *Al-Tirmidhi*, Number 602.

Summary of the Seven Earths

Muslim traditions often describe the earth as consisting of seven layers, each with unique characteristics and inhabitants:

1. **Ramaka**: Inhabited by the *Muwashshim*, who face eternal punishment.
2. **Khalada**: Home to torture devices for Hell's inhabitants.
3. **Arqa**: Populated by mule-like eagles with poisonous tails.
4. **Haraba**: Dwelling place of massive snakes with fangs like palm trees.
5. **Maltham**: A layer where sulfur stones torment the wicked.
6. **Sijjin**: The register of Hell's inhabitants.
7. **Ajiba**: The domain of Iblis (Satan) and the *Khasum*, a race destined to destroy Gog and Magog.

Source: *Qisas al-Anbiya* and *Tanwîr al-Miqbâs min Tafsîr Ibn 'Abbâs*.

Conclusion

The cosmological depictions in Islamic traditions blend spiritual insights with mythological imagery. These narratives, often rooted in early exegetical works, provide fascinating insights into how the universe's structure was perceived in Islamic thought. While many of these accounts are fantastical and symbolic, they have shaped theological discussions and interpretations within Islamic scholarship.

Summary of Islamic Cosmology Based on Early Traditions

And the earth was tossed about with its inhabitants like a ship, so God sent down an angel of extreme magnitude and strength **and ordered him to slip beneath the earth and bear it up on his shoulders. He stretched forth one of his hands to the East and the other to the West and took hold of the earth from end to end** [Note: this again presumes that the earth is flat]. However, there was no foothold for him, so God created from an emerald a square rock, in the middle of which were seven thousand holes. In each hole there was a sea, description of which is known only to God. **And He commanded the rock to settle beneath the angel's feet**. The rock, however, had no support, **so God created a great bull with forty thousand heads, eyes, ears, nostrils, mouths, tongues and legs and commanded it to bear the rock on its back and on its horns**. The name of the bull is al-Rayyan. As the bull had no place to rest its feet, **God created a huge fish, upon which no one may gaze because it is so enormous and had so many eyes**. It is even said that if all the seas were placed in one of its gills, they would be like a mustard seed in the desert. **This fish God commanded to be a foothold for the bull, and it was done**. The name of this fish is Behemoth. Then He made its resting place the waters, beneath which is the air, and beneath the air is the Darkness, which is for all the earths. There, beneath the Darkness, the knowledge of created things ends. (Ibid., translated by Wheeler M. Thackston Jr. [Great Books of the Islamic World, Inc., Distributed by Kazi Publications; Chicago, IL 1997], pp. 8-10; bold emphasis ours)

Foundational Beliefs from Early Islamic Narrations

1. **Earth on the Back of a Fish**:
    - According to early Islamic traditions, Allah created the earth and flattened it on the back of a giant fish (or whale).
    - The movement of this fish causes instability, which was mitigated by Allah creating mountains to act as stabilizers.
2. **Cosmic Layers**:

- o The fish floats in an otherworldly water.
- o Below the water lies a rock, which is supported by an angel standing on another rock.
- o This second rock is held up by wind, existing neither in the heavens nor on the earth.

3. **Seven Earths and Layers**:
   - o Some narrations state that the fish is beneath the seventh earth, and on its back rests a massive rock.
   - o An ox with 40,000 horns stands on this rock, supporting all seven earths.
   - o Other versions describe the ox as resting on the fish.

4. **Above the Earth**:
   - o There is a sea above the seventh heaven, with eight mountain goats above it.
   - o The throne of Allah exists above these cosmic layers.

Source: Narrations from *Tafsir Ibn Abbas*, *Al-Tabari*, and other classical Islamic commentators.

Comparison with Biblical Simplicity

The Biblical description of the earth and cosmos contrasts sharply with the complexity and mythology found in early Islamic traditions:

1. **The Earth and the Void**:
   - o "He stretches out the north over the void and hangs the earth on nothing." (*Job 26:7*)

2. **The Circle of the Earth**:
   - o "It is he who sits above the circle of the earth, and its inhabitants are like grasshoppers; who stretches out the heavens like a curtain, and spreads them like a tent to dwell in." (*Isaiah 40:22*)

These verses emphasize a simple yet profound understanding of creation.

A Contradiction in the Quran

1. **Earth Already Spread Out**:
   - The Quran often describes the earth as already spread out:
     - *"And He it is Who spread (madda) the earth and made in it firm mountains and rivers..." (Surah 13:3, Shakir)*
2. **Earth to Be Spread Out on Judgment Day**:
   - On the Day of Judgment, the Quran states that the earth will be spread out again:
     - *"And when the earth is spread out (muddat) and cast out all that is in her, and appears to become empty." (Surah 84:3-4, Sher Ali)*

Commentary by Ibn Kathir:

- Ibn Kathir interprets *Surah 84* to mean that the earth will be stretched out, expanded, and extended on the Day of Judgment. This is inconsistent with the claim that the earth is already spread out in the present.

Conclusion

These early Islamic traditions and Quranic descriptions present a cosmology influenced by mythology, often resembling Greek and Indian cosmological beliefs. The concepts of a flat earth supported by a giant fish or ox, along with mountains stabilizing the earth, align more with ancient folklore than with scientific understanding. Furthermore, the Quran's depiction of the earth being "spread out" now and again on Judgment Day introduces a contradiction regarding its current state.

In contrast, the Bible provides a clear and concise depiction of the earth, devoid of the mythical elements found in early Islamic thought.

CHAPTER 6

Are Mountains "Pegs" That Prevent the Earth from Shaking?

Introduction

The Qur'an mentions several times that Allah placed mountains on the earth to prevent it from shaking. These verses describe the role of mountains as stabilizing features:

- **Sura 16:15**:*"And He has set up on the earth mountains standing firm, lest it should shake with you; and rivers and roads; that ye may guide yourselves."*
- **Sura 21:31**:*"And We have set on the earth mountains standing firm, lest it should shake with them, and We have made therein broad highways (between mountains) for them to pass through: that they may receive Guidance."*
- **Sura 31:10**:*"He created the heavens without any pillars that ye can see; He set on the earth mountains standing firm, lest it should shake with you."*

- **Sura 78:7**:*"And the mountains as pegs?"*
- **Sura 79:32-33**:*"And the mountains hath He firmly fixed; for use and convenience to you and your cattle."*

Of these, **Sura 78:7** is the only verse that explicitly describes mountains as "pegs." The Qur'an does not directly mention mountains having "roots," but some Muslim apologists claim that the term "pegs" refers to the deep roots of mountains. This interpretation is often presented as evidence of the Qur'an's miraculous scientific foreknowledge, asserting that Muhammad could not have known about mountain roots without divine revelation.

Mountains in Ancient Knowledge

While this interpretation suggests a miraculous origin for the Qur'an's descriptions, the concept of mountain "roots" was already known in ancient times. For example, the Bible refers to the roots and foundations of mountains:

- **Job 28:9**:*"People assault the flinty rock with their hands and lay bare the roots of the mountains."*
- **Psalm 18:7**:*"The earth trembled and quaked, and the foundations of the mountains shook; they trembled because he was angry."*
- **Jonah 2:6**:*"To the roots of the mountains I sank down; the earth beneath barred me in forever. But you, LORD my God, brought my life up from the pit."*

These examples indicate that ancient people were aware of the concept of mountain foundations. Therefore, describing mountains as having roots or foundations was not unique to the Qur'an or unknown at the time.

Semantic Issues: Pegs vs. Roots

Equating "pegs" with "roots" presents a linguistic and conceptual problem. Pegs are artificial, human-made objects driven into the ground to hold things in place, such as tents. Roots, on the other hand, are naturally occurring and result from geological processes like the collision and subduction of tectonic plates.

Moreover, not all mountains have roots, especially volcanic mountains, which are formed by molten material rising to the earth's surface. Therefore, the comparison between roots and pegs is scientifically inaccurate and semantically flawed.

Interpretation and Purpose of the Verses

Some may view these Qur'anic verses as poetic or allegorical, reflecting the worldview of ancient people who may have believed in a flat earth, with mountains acting like paperweights to stabilize it. Others interpret the verses literally, ascribing a scientific significance to them and arguing that they prove the Qur'an's divine origin by describing concepts unknown in the 7th century.

A Google search for "mountains pegs miracle" yields thousands of results, demonstrating the popularity of this claim among some Muslim apologists.

Traditional Islamic Commentary

Historical Islamic interpretations often reflect the belief that mountains stabilize the earth. For instance, George Sale, cited by Wherry (*Answering Islam*), writes: *"The Muhammadans suppose that the earth, when first created, was smooth and equal, and thereby liable to a circular motion as well as the celestial orbs; and that the angels asking who could be able to stand on so tottering a frame, God fixed it the next morning by throwing the mountains on it."*

The **Tafsir al-Jalalayn** similarly explains: *"And the mountains pegs? With which the earth is tied down like tents are tied down with pegs."*

Conclusion

The claim that the Qur'an describes mountains as "pegs" to indicate their stabilizing "roots" is both scientifically and linguistically flawed. While mountains do have foundations due to geological processes, this knowledge was not unique to the Qur'an and was already present in ancient traditions, including the Bible. Furthermore, describing mountains as pegs misunderstands their natural formation and does not account for the differences between pegs and roots.

Instead of scientific insight, these verses likely reflect ancient cosmological views where mountains were imagined to stabilize a flat earth, a concept shared by many early civilizations. Thus, while the Qur'an's descriptions of mountains may be poetic or allegorical, they cannot be considered miraculous scientific knowledge.

Do Mountains Really Prevent the Earth from Shaking?

Introduction: The Qur'an's Claim

The Qur'an claims that mountains stabilize the earth and prevent it from shaking:

- **Sura 16:15**: *"And He has set up on the earth mountains standing firm, lest it should shake with you."*
- **Sura 21:31**: *"And We have set on the earth mountains standing firm, lest it should shake with them."*
- **Sura 31:10**: *"He set on the earth mountains standing firm, lest it should shake with you."*
- **Sura 78:7**: *"And the mountains as pegs?"*

The idea presented here is that mountains act as stabilizers or "pegs" to prevent earthquakes. However, this assertion faces significant factual and logical problems.

Factual Issues: Earthquakes and Mountains

The most glaring problem with this claim is that earthquakes occur every day, many in areas with prominent mountain ranges. A quick visit to the **United States Geological Survey (USGS)** website shows the global distribution of earthquakes. These often occur in regions with significant mountains, such as:

- Western North and South America
- The Aleutian Islands
- The Pacific "Ring of Fire"
- The Himalayas

Similarly, within the United States, earthquakes frequently happen in mountainous regions like the Rocky Mountains, the Cascades, and even the Appalachian Mountains.

Contrary to the Qur'anic implication, mountains are not placed on the earth to prevent earthquakes. Instead, they are *created* by tectonic activity—the very process responsible for earthquakes. For example:

- The collision of tectonic plates forms mountain ranges like the Himalayas.
- Subduction zones (where one tectonic plate slides beneath another) generate both volcanic activity and earthquakes, forming ranges like the Cascades.

The USGS map clearly shows that earthquakes often coincide with mountain regions, debunking the claim that mountains prevent seismic activity.

Logical Problems with the "Pegs" Analogy

The Qur'an describes mountains as "pegs," implying they stabilize the earth like tent pegs secure a tent. However, this analogy is logically flawed:

1. **Pegs Anchor Objects to Something Else**: A peg fixes an object to the ground. If mountains are "pegs," what exactly are they anchoring the earth to? To say they "peg" the earth to itself is nonsensical.
2. **Mountains as a Result of Plate Movement**: Mountains are the *effect* of tectonic activity, not the cause of stability. The very process that creates mountains—tectonic plate collisions—is responsible for earthquakes.

Counterclaims by Muslim Apologists

Some Muslim apologists argue that mountains stabilize tectonic plates and reduce the intensity of earthquakes. One apologist writes:

"Mountains hold tectonic plates together and buffer against earthquakes. While it's true that mountains are created by tectonic movement, once formed, they counteract seismic activity."

This argument misunderstands cause and effect. Mountains result from tectonic collisions and do not function as stabilizers for tectonic plates. Plate movements slow due to natural forces, not because of mountains.

Misuse of Scientific Sources

To support the claim that mountains act as pegs, some Muslim apologists misrepresent scientific texts. For example, they frequently cite the geology textbook **Earth** by Frank Press, often reproducing an illustration that shows mountains with deep roots. However, there are two major issues with their citation:

1. **Misplaced Reference**: The illustration they cite is from page 429, not page 413.
2. **Altered Text**: Muslim apologists have been known to replace the original caption with their own interpretation to fit their narrative. In reality, Frank Press does not describe mountains as "pegs" or claim that they prevent earthquakes.

The original illustration in **Earth** discusses mountain roots in the context of geological processes, not as stabilizers of tectonic activity.

Scientific Clarifications

The suggestion that mountains reduce earthquake severity in some regions is only partially accurate. For example, a scientific study cited by apologists mentions that the San Gabriel Mountains reduce the peak amplitude of certain seismic waves in Los Angeles. However:

- This effect is localized and does not mean the mountains prevent earthquakes.
- The study refers to surface wave scattering, not the role of mountains as "pegs."

Thus, while topography can influence seismic wave behavior in specific areas, mountains do not stabilize the earth or prevent earthquakes globally.

Conclusion: Misguided Claims

The Qur'anic claim that mountains act as pegs to prevent the earth from shaking is factually and logically flawed:

- Earthquakes frequently occur in mountainous regions.
- Mountains are formed by tectonic activity, which causes earthquakes.
- Describing mountains as "pegs" ignores the natural geological processes behind their formation.

Attempts to portray this claim as a scientific miracle rely on misinterpretation, misuse of sources, and conflation of unrelated concepts. The evidence overwhelmingly shows that the Qur'anic description of mountains as stabilizers does not align with scientific understanding.

Do Mountains Stabilize the Earth?

Understanding the Scientific Context

Professor Frank Press used an illustration in his book *Earth* to explain the principle of **isostasy**, which describes how the Earth's crust, including mountains, "floats" on the semi-fluid mantle below. The concept is akin to icebergs floating on water: the less dense crust sits atop the denser mantle. Here's an excerpt from his book (pages 428–429):

"The thickness of the crust varies from about 35 kilometers to 10 kilometers in a section extending from continent to ocean. Under a high mountain, the crust thickens to as much as 65 kilometers. If Figure 17-38 suggests to the reader that the continental crust floats on the denser mantle like an iceberg on the ocean, he has made a good observation... When Archimedes' principle of buoyancy is applied to the floatation of continents and mountains, it becomes the principle of isostasy."

Notably, **Professor Press does not say** that mountains stabilize the Earth or prevent earthquakes. Instead, he explains that the crust, including mountains, floats on the mantle, and its equilibrium is maintained through isostasy.

Misuse of Science by Muslim Apologists

Some Muslim apologists claim that the principle of isostasy proves the Qur'an's "scientific miracle" about mountains being "pegs." For example, one website states:

"The crust of the Earth floats on a liquid... The depths of the mountain strata go as far down as 35 km. Thus, the mountains are sort of pegs driven into the Earth. Just like pegs stabilize a tent on the ground, mountains stabilize the Earth's crust."

This analogy is flawed:

1. **Mountains Are Part of the Crust**: Mountains are not separate "pegs" driven into the crust; they are a part of it and float along with the crust on the mantle.
2. **Pegs vs. Floating**: Pegs fix something in place, but mountains, along with the crust, float on the mantle. A "floating peg" is an oxymoron—it cannot stabilize anything.
3. **Tectonic Activity**: Mountains are formed by tectonic activity, such as the collision of plates, which is also responsible for earthquakes. Far from preventing quakes, the processes that create mountains are the very cause of seismic activity.

The False Analogy of Mountains as Nails

Some apologists make the bizarre claim that:

"Mountains prevent the Earth's crust from sliding over the magma layer. In short, mountains can be compared to nails holding strips of wood together."

This claim contradicts the principle of isostasy, which describes the crust as floating on the mantle. Professor Press explicitly states that the crust floats on a semi-fluid layer, making it impossible for mountains to act as nails fixing the crust in place.

Misrepresentation of Scientific Texts

Muslim websites frequently misrepresent scientific texts to fit their narrative. For instance, they cite Andrae Cailleux's *Anatomy of the Earth*, altering the caption of an image to claim:

"The mountains, like pegs, have deep roots embedded in the ground."

However, the original caption in Cailleux's book does not describe mountains as pegs or mention stabilization. Instead, it explains geological processes without aligning them with Qur'anic claims. Such manipulation undermines the credibility of these arguments.

Conclusion

The idea that mountains stabilize the Earth or prevent earthquakes is scientifically inaccurate and unsupported by credible evidence. Instead:

1. Mountains are part of the Earth's crust, which floats on the mantle due to isostasy.
2. Tectonic activity, which forms mountains, is the primary cause of earthquakes.

3. Misrepresentation of scientific texts and concepts to fit a religious narrative is dishonest and counterproductive.

If the Qur'an is truly the "truth," as Muslims believe, why resort to altering facts or fabricating evidence to prove its validity? Intellectual honesty requires presenting facts as they are, not manipulating them to fit preconceived notions.

C H A P T E R 7

Islamic Dishonesty and the Claim of Earth's Rotation in the Quran

Introduction

Achieving success at the cost of honesty is a hollow victory, often worse than failure itself. Unfortunately, some modern Islamic scholars and commentators resort to fabrications and pseudo-miracles to present the Qur'an as a scientifically miraculous text. By distorting their scripture through misinterpretation, these scholars aim to convince their audience, who are often predisposed to believe in the Qur'an's miraculous nature. This manipulation is frequently motivated by the desire for material or social gain.

Such distortions arise from several sources: ignorance of the verse's historical and linguistic context, isolating it from related passages, and deliberate neglect of Arabic grammatical nuances to mislead those unfamiliar with the language. Ironically, Muhammad himself accused the Jews of his time of distorting their scriptures (Surah 2:75, Surah 3:78). Yet today, many Muslim propagandists are guilty of doing the same with their own sacred text—fabricating so-called miracles and undermining their credibility.

This study examines a prominent miracle claim about the Qur'an allegedly revealing the Earth's rotation. We will expose the dishonesty in these claims by analyzing their flawed logic and misrepresentations.

Section I: Halûk Nurbaki's Pseudo-Miracle – The Rotation of the Earth

In his book, *Verses From the Glorious Koran and the Facts of Science*, Turkish Islamic commentator Dr. Halûk Nurbaki argues that the Qur'an miraculously describes the Earth's rotation. He bases his claim on this verse:

"You see the mountains and think them jamid (lifeless, motionless); yet they progress, just as clouds progress. Such is the handiwork of God, who has disposed of everything in firmness. He is completely aware of all you do." (*Surah 27:88*, as cited by Nurbaki, p. 73)

Nurbaki interprets the verse as implying that mountains move spatially, an indirect reference to the Earth's rotation. He claims the comparison of mountains to clouds suggests the Earth itself is in motion. He praises the Qur'an for presenting this concept 14 centuries ago, allegedly demonstrating its divine origin (p. 77).

Problems with Nurbaki's Interpretation

1. **Contradictions with Other Verses** While Nurbaki claims the Qur'an describes the Earth's rotation, other verses explicitly deny any motion of the Earth or heavens. For example:

"Lo! Allah graspeth the heavens and the earth that they deviate not, and if they were to deviate there is not one that could grasp them after Him. Lo! He is ever Clement, Forgiving." (*Surah 35:41*, Pickthall)

This verse suggests the Earth and heavens are fixed in place and would only move if Allah allowed it—directly contradicting the idea of an Earth in constant rotation.

2. **The Qur'an's Description of Mountains** Numerous Qur'anic verses describe mountains as "firmly fixed," emphasizing their stability:

   - "And He it is Who spread the earth and made in it firm mountains and rivers..." (*Surah 13:3*, Shakir)
   - "And the mountains hath He firmly fixed." (*Surah 79:32*, Yusuf Ali)
   - "Or, Who has made the earth firm to live in; made rivers in its midst; set thereon mountains immovable..." (*Surah 27:61*, Yusuf Ali)
   - "And the earth – We have spread it forth and made in it firm mountains..." (*Surah 15:19*, Shakir)

These verses portray mountains as static and immovable features of the Earth, contradicting Nurbaki's interpretation of their movement.

3. **Misuse of the Word *Jamid*** The word *jamid* in *Surah 27:88* means "motionless" or "lifeless." Nurbaki's claim hinges on the idea that the mountains' perceived stillness is an illusion, as they are moving with the Earth's rotation. However, this reading is far from the intended meaning of the verse, which is poetic and likely refers to the eventual upheaval of mountains on Judgment Day, a theme recurrent in the Qur'an.

The Context of Qur'anic Cosmology

Nurbaki's argument is further weakened by the Qur'an's broader depiction of cosmology, which reflects the prevailing geocentric worldview of the 7th century. Verses describe the Earth as spread out flat and mountains as stabilizing pegs holding the Earth in place.

For instance:

"He created the heavens without any pillars that ye can see; He set on the earth mountains standing firm, lest it should shake with you..." (*Surah 31:10*, Yusuf Ali)

This verse implies that mountains prevent the Earth from shaking—a belief inconsistent with modern geological science, which shows that mountains are a result of tectonic activity and do not stabilize the Earth.

Conclusion

Dr. Halûk Nurbaki's claim that the Qur'an describes the Earth's rotation is unconvincing and riddled with contradictions. His interpretation isolates a single verse from its broader context and ignores other verses that emphasize the Earth's stability.

The Qur'an's descriptions of cosmology align more closely with the ancient, pre-scientific worldview of a flat, immobile Earth. Attempts to retroactively impose modern scientific concepts onto the Qur'an often involve significant misinterpretation or dishonesty. Such claims not only fail to substantiate the Qur'an's divine origin but also undermine the credibility of its proponents.

Honesty and intellectual rigor should take precedence over efforts to fabricate miracles in sacred texts. If the Qur'an is truly a divine revelation, it should stand on its own merits without the need for misleading interpretations.

The Role of Mountains in the Qur'an: A Rebuttal to the Earth's Rotation Claim

Mountains as Firm Structures

The Qur'an describes mountains as firm structures established by Allah to stabilize the earth and prevent it from shaking. Consider the following verses:

- **"He set on the (earth), mountains standing firm, high above it, and bestowed blessings on the earth, and measured therein all things to give them nourishment in due proportion, in four Days, in accordance with (the needs of) those who seek (Sustenance)."** (*Surah 41:10*, Yusuf Ali)
- **"And He has set up on the earth mountains standing firm, lest it should shake with you; and rivers and roads; that ye may guide yourselves."** (*Surah 16:15*, Yusuf Ali)
- **"Have We not made the earth as a wide expanse, and the mountains as pegs?"** (*Surah 78:6-7*, Yusuf Ali)
- **"He created the heavens without pillars that ye can see, and He threw upon the earth firm mountains lest it should move with you; and He dispersed thereon every sort of beast; and We send down from the heavens water, and We caused to grow therein of every noble kind."** (*Surah 31:10*, Palmer)
- **"And We have set on the earth mountains standing firm, lest it should shake with them, and We have made therein broad highways (between mountains) for them to pass through: that they may receive Guidance."** (*Surah 21:31*, Yusuf Ali)

These verses clearly depict mountains as immovable structures, integral to the earth's stability, and preventing it from shaking. This concept reveals a scientifically inaccurate understanding of mountains' nature and purpose.

Contradictions in the Qur'anic Perspective

This view of mountains as stabilizers directly contradicts the claim made by some modern Muslim apologists, such as Dr. Halûk Nurbaki, that *Surah 27:88* implies the earth's rotation.

- **"You see the mountains and think them jamid (lifeless, motionless); yet they progress, just as clouds progress. Such is the handiwork of God, who has disposed of everything in firmness. He is completely aware of all you do."** (*Surah 27:88*)

While Nurbaki interprets this verse to suggest that mountains move due to the Earth's rotation, the broader Qur'anic context emphasizes the mountains' immobility and their role in stabilizing the earth. The contradiction is stark: the Qur'an cannot simultaneously claim that mountains stabilize the earth and that they move due to the Earth's rotation.

Mountains and Motion: Present vs. Future

Interestingly, some verses in the Qur'an do describe mountains in motion, but these references consistently pertain to the future—specifically, the Day of Judgment:

- **"When the sun is folded up, and when the stars are obscured, and when the mountains are made to move."** (*Surah 81:1-3*, Sher Ali)
- **"The day when there shall be a blast on the trumpet, and ye shall come in crowds, and the heaven shall be opened**

and be full of portals, and the mountains shall be set in motion, and melt into thin vapor.” (*Surah 78:18-20*, Rodwell)

- **“On the day when the heaven will heave with (awful) heaving, and the mountains move away with (awful) movement.”** (*Surah 52:9-10*, Pickthall)

- **“Then when the Trumpet will be blown with one blowing (the first one), and the earth with the mountains shall be lifted up and crushed with one crash.”** (*Surah 69:13-14*, Pickthall)

These verses describe cataclysmic events during the end times, emphasizing the extraordinary upheaval that will occur. They do not, in any way, support the notion of a continuous, systematic motion of mountains corresponding to the Earth's rotation.

If the Qur'an indeed acknowledged the Earth's rotation, it would not consistently depict mountains as markers of the present Earth's stability while reserving their motion as a future, extraordinary event.

Mountains as Signs of Miracles

The Qur'an further reinforces the mountains' immobility by associating their movement with a miraculous event capable of proving divine authority:

- **“If there were a Qur'an with which mountains were moved, or the earth were cloven asunder, or the dead were made to speak, (this would be the one!) But, truly, the command is with God in all things!”** (*Surah 13:31*, Yusuf Ali)

This verse highlights that the movement of mountains is considered an impossibility in the present order of creation, further contradicting the idea that the Qur'an hints at the Earth's rotation.

Conclusion

The Qur'an consistently portrays mountains as immovable structures, stabilizing the earth and preventing it from shaking. While some modern commentators claim that *Surah 27:88* suggests the Earth's rotation, this interpretation is incompatible with the Qur'an's repeated emphasis on the mountains' firmness and their association with the earth's stability.

Moreover, the Qur'an's descriptions of mountains in motion are explicitly linked to the apocalyptic upheaval of the Day of Judgment, not to any present or ongoing phenomenon such as the Earth's rotation. Attempts to align the Qur'an with modern scientific discoveries often result in cherry-picking verses and ignoring the broader context, leading to contradictory interpretations.

As such, claims of scientific miracles in the Qur'an lack textual basis and should be critically evaluated within the framework of both historical context and modern scientific understanding.

Context of Surah 27:88: Analyzing Its Meaning and Implications

Nurbaki's Interpretation in Context

Dr. Halûk Nurbaki claims that *Surah 27:88* demonstrates the Qur'an's awareness of the Earth's rotation. However, a closer examination of the verse in its immediate and broader context reveals that this interpretation is far-fetched and inconsistent with the Qur'anic narrative. The verse reads:

"And thou seest the mountains, which thou thinkest to be firmly fixed, pass away as the clouds pass away - the handiwork of Allah, who has made everything perfect. Verily, He is fully aware of what you do." (*Surah 27:88*, Sher Ali)

When we consider the surrounding verses, the meaning becomes clear:

- **"And call to mind the day when the trumpet will be blown, and whoever is in the heavens and whoever is in the earth will be struck with terror, save him whom Allah pleases. And all shall come unto Him humbled."** (*Surah 27:87*, Sher Ali)

- **"Whoever does a good deed shall have a better reward than that, and such will be secure from terror that day. And those who do evil shall be thrown down on their faces into the Fire; and it will be said to them, 'Are you not rewarded for what you have been doing?'"** (*Surah 27:89-90*, Sher Ali)

These verses place *Surah 27:88* firmly within the eschatological context of the Day of Judgment. The mention of mountains "passing away" refers not to their movement due to Earth's rotation but rather to their destruction during the end times, as described in numerous other Qur'anic verses.

The final phrase of *Surah 27:88*, **"Verily, He is fully aware of what you do,"** aligns seamlessly with the preceding and following verses, emphasizing accountability for human deeds on the Day of Judgment. This reinforces the eschatological theme, rendering Nurbaki's interpretation misplaced and inconsistent with the text.

Comparison with Other Verses on Mountains and Judgment Day

The idea of mountains being set in motion is reiterated in other Qur'anic passages, always in the context of the Day of Judgment:

- **"They ask thee concerning the mountains: say, 'My Lord will uproot them and scatter them as dust; He will leave them as plains smooth and level; nothing crooked or curved wilt thou see in their place.' On that Day will they follow the Caller (straight): no crookedness (can they show) him."** (*Surah 20:105-108*, Yusuf Ali)

These verses emphasize that mountains, considered symbols of stability, will be utterly destroyed on the Day of Judgment. The analogy in *Surah 27:88*, likening mountains to clouds, aligns with other metaphors used to describe their eventual dispersal, such as being compared to **"scattered wool"** (*Surah 70:9, Surah 101:5*) or **"heaps of sand"** (*Surah 73:14*).

Metaphor or Misinterpretation?

Nurbaki's interpretation of *Surah 27:88* as a reference to Earth's rotation misreads the analogy between mountains and clouds. The comparison aims to evoke imagery of mountains being effortlessly displaced, emphasizing divine power. It does not suggest that mountains move due to Earth's rotation.

The claim further collapses when contrasted with *Surah 24:43*, where clouds themselves are referred to as "mountains" containing hail:

"Hast thou not seen how Allah wafteth the clouds, then gathereth them, then maketh them layers, and thou seest the rain come forth from between them; He sendeth down from the heaven mountains wherein is hail." (*Surah 24:43*, Pickthall)

This shows the Qur'an's use of descriptive language and metaphors to convey ideas, which should not be confused with scientific explanations.

Conclusion: No Scientific Basis

When *Surah 27:88* is read within its context, it becomes evident that it describes a future event tied to the Day of Judgment rather than Earth's present rotation. The analogy of mountains passing away as clouds serves to underscore the dramatic upheaval of the end times, not to suggest scientific insight into Earth's movement.

By isolating the verse and applying modern scientific concepts, interpreters like Nurbaki remove it from its eschatological context and attribute meanings unsupported by the text. Far from being evidence of a "scientific miracle," *Surah 27:88* aligns with the broader Qur'anic theme of divine power and the final judgment.

Grammatical Issues in Interpreting Surah 27:88

Islamic apologists, such as Dr. Halûk Nurbaki, often highlight certain verses in the Qur'an as supposedly aligning with scientific facts. However, their interpretations frequently rely on misreading or misunderstanding grammatical nuances in the Qur'anic text. One key issue is the use of the *present tense* in Arabic, which often leads to misconceptions when interpreted literally.

For instance, the argument that *Surah 27:88* references Earth's rotation hinges on the verse's present tense:

"And thou seest the mountains, which thou thinkest to be firmly fixed, pass away as the clouds pass away - the handiwork of Allah Who has made everything perfect. Verily, He is fully aware of what you do." (*Surah 27:88*, Pickthall)

Some translators modify the verbs to the *future tense* to align with the eschatological context of the verse. Compare various translations:

- **Pickthall:** *"And thou seest the hills thou deemest solid flying with the flight of clouds: the doing of Allah Who perfecteth all things. Lo! He is Informed of what ye do."*
- **Yusuf Ali:** *"Thou seest the mountains and thinkest them firmly fixed: but they shall pass away as the clouds pass away..."*
- **Hilali-Khan:** *"And you will see the mountains and think them solid, but they shall pass away as the passing away of the clouds..."*

- **Arberry:** *"And thou shalt see the mountains, that thou supposest fixed, passing by like clouds..."*

The variation in translations highlights the effort of some scholars to render the tense in a way that reflects the eschatological nature of the verse. While the original Arabic employs present tense, the future tense in these translations acknowledges the broader context, particularly the Day of Judgment.

Arabic Grammar and Context

Arabic often uses the present tense to describe future events, especially when discussing eschatological or prophetic occurrences. This grammatical feature can cause confusion when translated literally. For example, compare the structure of *Surah 27:88* with *Surah 39:75*, another verse about the Day of Judgment:

Surah 39:75 (Pickthall): *"And thou (O Muhammad) seest the angels thronging round the Throne, hymning the praises of their Lord. And they are judged aright. And it is said: Praise be to Allah, the Lord of the Worlds!"*

Arabic transliteration: *Watara almala-ikata haffeena min hawli alAAarshi yusabbihoona bihamdi rabbihim waqudiya baynahum bialhaqqi waqeela alhamdu lillahi rabbi alAAalameena*

Here, Yusuf Ali translates the verbs into future tense to reflect the eschatological nature of the verse:

"And thou wilt see the angels surrounding the Throne (Divine) on all sides, singing Glory and Praise to their Lord..." (*Surah 39:75*, Yusuf Ali).

This change makes the meaning clearer in English and avoids confusion. The passage is about events on the Day of Judgment, which are yet to occur. The same logic applies to *Surah 27:88*. The context provided by adjacent verses, such as *Surah 27:87*, which mentions the blowing of the trumpet signaling the Day of Judgment, confirms that the mountains "passing away like clouds" refers to future events.

Misinterpretation and Contextual Isolation

Apologists like Nurbaki often isolate *Surah 27:88* from its surrounding verses, allowing them to impose an interpretation that aligns with modern science. However, the immediate context makes it clear that the verse describes the end times:

- **Surah 27:87 (Sher Ali):** *"And call to mind the day when the trumpet will be blown and whoever is in the heavens and whoever is in the earth will be struck with terror…"*
- **Surah 27:89-90 (Sher Ali):** *"Whoever does a good deed shall have a better reward… And those who do evil shall be thrown down on their faces into the Fire."*

The consistent eschatological tone of these verses reinforces that the mountains' movement is a future event tied to the Day of Judgment.

Analogous Verses Supporting Future Interpretation

Another example of a similar grammatical structure is *Surah 39:68*, which describes events on the Day of Judgment using present tense in Arabic but is often rendered in the future tense in English:

"And the trumpet is blown, and all who are in the heavens and all who are in the earth swoon away, save him whom Allah willeth. Then it is blown a second time, and behold them standing waiting!" (*Surah 39:68*, Pickthall).

This grammatical pattern confirms that the Qur'anic author frequently uses present tense to describe future events, underscoring that *Surah 27:88* should be understood in the same way.

Conclusion

The claim that *Surah 27:88* references Earth's rotation relies on isolating the verse from its context and misunderstanding Arabic grammar. The verse does not describe current phenomena but future events tied to the Day of Judgment. Translators who render the verbs in the future tense do so to align with the eschatological context, not to distort the Qur'an.

By contextualizing *Surah 27:88* and comparing it to similar passages, it becomes clear that it does not support any scientific insights about Earth's rotation. Instead, it reinforces the Qur'an's consistent portrayal of the Day of Judgment.

Clarification of Surah 27:88 in Context

A Related Verse: Surah 18:47

A verse closely resembling Surah 27:88 in both theme and structure is:

"And (bethink you of) the Day when We remove the hills and you see the earth emerging, and We gather them together so as to leave not one of them behind." (*Surah 18:47, Pickthall*)

Arabic transliteration: *Wayawma nusayyiru aljibala watara al-arda barizatan wahasharnahum falam nughadir minhum ahadan.*

How might proponents of miraculous interpretations, such as Halûk Nurbaki, explain this verse? If interpreted literally, it suggests that people can observe mountains being removed and the earth becoming flat in real-time. Since such events have never occurred, should this verse be considered a failed prophecy? Or does this reflect the limitations of Arabic, which lacks a distinct future tense, and the challenges of literal translation?

What's more revealing is the inconsistency among translators. While some maintain the *present tense* in *Surah 27:88*, they use *future tense* for the same verb form in *Surah 18:47*. Compare these examples:

- **Surah 18:47 (Khalifa):** *"The day will come when we wipe out the mountains, and you will see the earth barren. We will summon them all, not leaving out a single one of them."*
- **Surah 27:88 (Khalifa):** *"When you look at the mountains, you think that they are standing still. But they are moving, like the clouds..."*

The Arabic verb *tara* (translated as "see") appears identically in both verses. If it implies future events in *Surah 18:47* due to its reference to "the Day," why ignore that *Surah 27:88* follows *Surah 27:87*, which also refers to the Day of Judgment?

"And (remind them of) the Day when the Trumpet will be blown, and all who are in the heavens and the earth will start in fear, save him whom Allah willeth. And all come unto Him, humbled." (*Surah 27:87, Pickthall*)

Questions About the Miracle Claim

When the context of *Surah 27:88* is analyzed, it becomes clear that Nurbaki's claim about Earth's rotation is unfounded. However, several additional questions challenge his interpretation:

1. **Why focus only on mountains?** If the verse intended to imply Earth's rotation, why mention only mountains? The Earth's rotation affects rivers, valleys, lakes, oceans, and all other

features of the planet's surface equally. There is no logical reason to single out mountains as evidence of rotation.

2. **Faulty analogy with clouds:** Nurbaki's comparison of the movement of mountains to clouds is scientifically inaccurate. Clouds move independently, relative to the Earth's surface. In contrast, mountains move only *with* the Earth's surface as part of its rotation. Mountains do not glide "over the earth" like clouds. If the Qur'an had described the mountains moving in a different manner, such as in relation to tectonic shifts, it might have been more plausible. However, stating that mountains move "just as clouds do" is a scientific error.

3. **Observable movement:** If the Qur'an intended to describe the constant movement of mountains due to Earth's rotation, why use clouds as an analogy? The movement of clouds is observable, while the supposed motion of mountains is not visible to the human eye. This lack of clarity undermines the argument that the verse reveals Earth's rotation.

Conclusion

The context of *Surah 27:88* and related verses, such as *Surah 18:47*, reveals that the Qur'an describes events tied to the Day of Judgment, not the present motion of Earth or its rotation. The analogy of mountains and clouds, while poetic, is scientifically flawed when used to suggest constant motion.

Nurbaki's interpretation, which seeks to align this verse with modern scientific knowledge, misrepresents the text. The Qur'an's author describes mountains as stationary or as moving only during apocalyptic events, reinforcing that the verse does not address Earth's rotation. Ultimately, the claim that *Surah 27:88* is a miraculous reference to Earth's motion is both contextually and scientifically baseless.

Section II: Rebuttal to Websites Promoting the Pseudo-Miracle of Earth's Rotation

The claim that the Qur'an revealed the rotation of the Earth over a thousand years ago continues to gain traction among some Islamic scholars and commentators. While this assertion, popularized by figures like Halûk Nurbaki, relies on misinterpretations, others, such as Caner Taslaman and certain websites like *quranmiracles.com*, perpetuate similar claims with slight variations. Their shared methodology—distorting the text and its meaning—makes the rebuttal to Nurbaki equally relevant. However, the additional fallacies and assertions presented on these platforms merit further critique.

The Claim: The Earth's Rotation Implied in Surah 27:88

Caner Taslaman, the author of *The Quran, The Unchallengeable Miracle*, introduces his argument with the following assertion: *"The mountains' features seem to make them the most stationary components of the earth's surface. The idea of the unattainability of mountains led certain primitive mentalities to believe in polytheism and fancy that the mountains were the abode of divinities. The idea of mountain peaks being beyond man's reach was an illusion, as was also their stationary aspect."*

Taslaman uses Surah 27:88 to argue that the Qur'an dismissed the misconception of stationary mountains by suggesting their motion, similar to clouds. He claims this movement indicates the Earth's rotation, a concept unknown to people at the time of Muhammad. However, this interpretation leads to a glaring contradiction:

- The Qur'an contains multiple verses that describe mountains as stationary, serving as pegs to stabilize the Earth (*e.g., Surah 16:15, Surah 21:31, Surah 31:10*).
- If Taslaman's interpretation is applied consistently, the Qur'an simultaneously promotes a fixed and rotating Earth, a clear contradiction.

The Claim's Flaws

Misrepresentation of the Audience's Understanding

Taslaman asserts that the people of Muhammad's time misunderstood the verse because its scientific implications were beyond their grasp. This raises critical questions:

1. **If the Qur'an is intended to be a clear and universal guide, why would it contain information incomprehensible to its original audience?**
2. **Why would Muhammad, as the prophet responsible for explaining the Qur'an, fail to clarify the verse's supposed scientific meaning?**

The traditional commentaries on Surah 27:88, including those by esteemed scholars like Ibn Kathir, do not support Taslaman's interpretation. Instead, they consistently describe the verse as referring to the Day of Judgment, when mountains will be set in motion as part of the apocalyptic upheaval. Ibn Kathir comments:

"You will see them as if they are fixed... but they will pass away as the passing of clouds, i.e., they will move away from their places." (*Source: tafsir.com*)

This aligns with other verses describing the destruction of mountains on the Last Day (*e.g., Surah 20:105-107, Surah 18:47*). Thus, neither Muhammad nor early Muslim scholars interpreted this verse as referring to Earth's rotation.

The Baseless Authority of Modern Propagandists

Taslaman and other modern interpreters, such as Nurbaki and Harun Yahya, claim to have uncovered a scientific truth hidden in the Qur'an that eluded Muhammad and early commentators. This raises another critical question:

- **What qualifies these individuals to reinterpret the Qur'an and claim access to divine insight unavailable to earlier generations?**

If the verse indeed contains hidden scientific knowledge, it would imply that Muhammad and his contemporaries failed in their duty to interpret the Qur'an correctly. This undermines the core Islamic belief in the Qur'an's clarity and Muhammad's role as its ultimate interpreter.

Further Misinterpretations

The argument also hinges on a flawed analogy between mountains and clouds. Taslaman asserts that the verse implies Earth's rotation by likening mountain motion to that of clouds. However, this analogy is scientifically inaccurate:

- Clouds move independently of the Earth's surface, whereas mountains are fixed to the crust and move *with* it due to tectonic activity or Earth's rotation.
- If the Qur'an intended to reference Earth's rotation, why focus exclusively on mountains rather than include all terrestrial features, which rotate uniformly?

A Problematic Comparison

Surah 27:88 is similar to another verse, Surah 18:47, which also describes mountains in motion: *"And (bethink you of) the Day when We remove the hills and you see the earth emerging, and We gather them together so as to leave not one of them behind."* (*Surah 18:47, Pickthall*)

The verb *tara* ("you see") appears in the same form in both verses. Translators often interpret it as present tense in Surah 27:88 but future tense in Surah 18:47. This inconsistency highlights the importance of context, as Surah 27:87 explicitly references the Day of Judgment, linking it to the motion of mountains in the subsequent verse.

Conclusion

The claim that Surah 27:88 reveals Earth's rotation collapses under scrutiny. Traditional commentaries, context, and the Qur'an's own descriptions of mountains contradict Taslaman's interpretation. The comparison to clouds, while poetic, is scientifically flawed, and the verse itself refers to eschatological events, not present-day phenomena.

Finally, the selective reinterpretation of Qur'anic verses by modern propagandists undermines the Qur'an's coherence and clarity. If the Qur'an is indeed divine, it should not require distortion to align with modern science. Instead of proving the Qur'an's miraculous nature, such claims expose the lengths to which some will go to defend indefensible positions.

Taslaman's Faulty Interpretation and Misrepresentation

Taslaman's claim that Surah 27:88 implies the Earth's rotation is not only baseless but also contradicts the Qur'an's frequent emphasis on the immovability of mountains. His interpretation introduces an unwarranted notion of "illusion" into the text, deviating from its original meaning.

Key Issues in Taslaman's Argument

1. **Forcing the Concept of Illusion** Taslaman argues that the verse highlights an "illusion" regarding the stationary nature of mountains, implying their motion reflects the Earth's rotation. However, this claim introduces a term that does not exist in the original Arabic text. The verse's language does not suggest or support the concept of illusion.

2. **Pronoun Usage** Taslaman overlooks a critical grammatical detail: the verse uses a singular pronoun initially to describe an individual's observation but shifts to a plural pronoun when addressing humanity as a whole. This shift clearly indicates that the verse first focuses on an individual's perception and then transitions to a universal reminder of God's omniscience.

3. **Misinterpretation of Context** Taslaman's argument disregards the broader context of Surah 27:88 and similar verses in the Qur'an. By isolating the verse, he fails to acknowledge its alignment with other eschatological verses describing the Day of Judgment. For instance: *"And (bethink you of) the Day when we remove the hills, and you see the earth emerging, and We gather them together so as to leave not one of them behind."* (*Surah 18:47, Pickthall*)

The connection between Surah 27:88 and these verses demonstrates that the "movement" of mountains is a future event tied to the apocalypse, not a reference to Earth's present rotation.

A Contradictory Revelation

If Taslaman's interpretation is valid, it creates a contradiction within the Qur'an itself. Numerous verses emphasize that mountains are firm and stationary, serving as pegs to stabilize the Earth (*e.g., Surah 16:15, Surah 13:3, Surah 21:31*). Accepting Taslaman's claim would render these verses inconsistent with his supposed revelation of the Earth's rotation.

Flawed Assumptions and Misuse of Science

Taslaman's Analogy: Mountains and Clouds

Taslaman compares the motion of mountains to that of clouds, suggesting both imply the Earth's rotation. This analogy is scientifically flawed. Clouds move independently relative to the Earth's surface, while mountains are fixed to the crust and move only as part of the Earth's motion. To equate the two demonstrates a misunderstanding of basic geological principles.

Selective Interpretation

Taslaman conveniently focuses on mountains, ignoring that Earth's rotation would affect all features equally—valleys, rivers, forests, and oceans. If the Qur'an truly intended to describe the Earth's rotation, it would not single out mountains.

Historical and Theological Inconsistencies

Taslaman's assertion that earlier generations failed to grasp the supposed scientific meaning of this verse raises critical questions:

1. **Muhammad's Role** If the verse contains hidden scientific knowledge, why didn't Muhammad or early Muslim scholars explain it? Muhammad's role as a prophet included clarifying the Qur'an's meaning. The absence of such an explanation suggests that the verse was not understood, even by its original audience, to imply Earth's rotation.

2. **Ibn Kathir's Commentary** Esteemed commentator Ibn Kathir interpreted the verse as describing the apocalyptic upheaval of mountains on the Day of Judgment: *"You will see them as if they are fixed... but they will pass away as the passing of clouds."* (*Source: tafsir.com*)

This traditional interpretation is consistent with the Qur'an's eschatological narrative but contradicts modern miracle claims.

Broader Implications

Mixing Personal Ideas with Scripture

Taslaman criticizes those who mix human ideas with divine revelation, yet his interpretation does exactly that. He projects his own scientific understanding onto the Qur'an, distorting its intended meaning.

Fabricated Miracles and Intellectual Dishonesty

Modern commentators like Taslaman perpetuate pseudo-miracles by distorting the Qur'an to align with scientific discoveries. This intellectual dishonesty undermines the credibility of their arguments and disrespects the text they claim to defend.

Historical Parallels

Taslaman's reference to Galileo and the Church's opposition to heliocentrism illustrates the tension between religion and science. However, his subjective distinction between "original" and "fabricated" religion fails to address the reality that even true representatives of a faith can misinterpret or distort its teachings.

Conclusion

Taslaman's interpretation of Surah 27:88 as evidence of Earth's rotation is baseless, scientifically flawed, and contradictory to the Qur'an's broader narrative. His selective reading, misrepresentation of context, and flawed analogies reveal a pattern of intellectual dishonesty aimed at fabricating miracles.

Rather than clarifying the Qur'an, Taslaman's approach distorts it, undermining its coherence and the credibility of its defenders. Honest readers must reject such pseudo-miracles and focus on genuine, contextually accurate interpretations of religious texts.

A Related Pseudo-Miracle: Mountains in Motion

After presenting his interpretation of Surah 27:88, Caner Taslaman attempts to fabricate yet another pseudo-miracle from the same verse, claiming it reveals the concept of the Earth's continental drift.

Taslaman's Argument

Taslaman posits:

"The terrestrial crust moves as if floating on the denser mantle. This movement led to the separation of continents, once a unified landmass. German meteorologist and geologist Alfred Wegener proposed the theory of continental drift in 1915, which was later validated. Mountains, seemingly stationary to us, actually move along with the Earth's crust. This verse demonstrates the perfection of God's design." *(Source: quranmiracles.com)*

Taslaman expands on this, mentioning Earth's rotation, revolution, and complex movements within the solar system, suggesting these phenomena are described in the Qur'an. He concludes that the verse in Surah 27:88 reflects the undeniable brilliance of divine creation.

The Reality

Despite Taslaman's lengthy and enthusiastic exposition, his claims are fundamentally flawed. Nowhere does the Qur'an mention continental drift, nor does it imply that mountains are in constant motion as part of Earth's crust. In fact, the Qur'an repeatedly describes mountains as **firm** and **stationary**, with motion attributed to them only in the eschatological context of the Day of Judgment. Consider the following verse:

"Had it been possible for a Lecture to cause the mountains to move, or the earth to be torn asunder, or the dead to speak, (this Qur'an would have done so). Nay, but Allah's is the whole command." *(Surah 13:31, Pickthall)*

If the Qur'an truly acknowledged the concept of continental drift, the movement of mountains would not have been presented as miraculous or extraordinary. Instead, the verse reflects a belief in the impossibility of such movement, contradicting modern scientific discoveries.

A Contradictory Claim About Mountains

On his website, Taslaman also highlights another supposed miracle:

"The Qur'an describes mountains as pegs, which aligns with geological findings of recent centuries. Mountains rest on deep roots extending far beneath the surface. For example, Mount Everest, with a peak 9 km above ground, has a root extending approximately 125 km below. This depth stabilizes the Earth's crust, a phenomenon unknown during the Prophet's time." *(Source: quranmiracles.com)*

The Contradiction

This claim directly conflicts with Taslaman's earlier assertion that mountains are in motion like clouds. How can mountains stabilize the Earth if they are constantly moving? Describing mountains as "pegs" while simultaneously claiming they are mobile is a glaring contradiction. Did the Qur'an's author intend for us to believe in **moving pegs**?

Misleading Interpretations

The claim that mountains function as pegs stabilizing the Earth is also scientifically inaccurate. While mountains do have deep roots that extend into the mantle, this is a natural consequence of plate tectonics. Their presence does not "stabilize" the Earth's crust but is rather a byproduct of tectonic activity.

Taslaman further distorts facts by attributing geological concepts, such as the Earth's crust, to the Qur'an—a term and concept never mentioned in the text. His reliance on sources like *Earth* by Frank Press is similarly misleading. Press's description of mountains as wedges or roots refers to their structure, not their function as stabilizers. Taslaman's extrapolation is a deliberate attempt to force scientific ideas onto unrelated Qur'anic verses.

Scientific Reality vs. Qur'anic Claims

Mountains do not stabilize the Earth's crust. Instead, the Earth's crust floats on the mantle, with mountains forming due to the movement of tectonic plates. This movement—causing earthquakes and the formation of mountain ranges—contradicts the Qur'anic claim that mountains prevent the Earth from shaking. Taslaman's efforts to reconcile these facts with Qur'anic verses result in logical and factual inconsistencies.

The Misuse of Analogies

Taslaman likens mountains to tent pegs, suggesting they hold the Earth's crust in place. However, this analogy is flawed:

1. **Mountains are not "driven into" the Earth** but are formed through tectonic processes.

2. If mountains were pegs that stabilized the Earth, the frequent occurrence of earthquakes—especially in mountainous regions—would not align with this claim.

3. Taslaman conflates the metaphorical language of ancient texts with scientific accuracy, misleading readers into believing the Qur'an anticipated modern geology.

Conclusion

Taslaman's claims about mountains in motion and their supposed role as stabilizers are contradictory and lack scientific basis. By selectively interpreting Qur'anic verses and forcing modern scientific concepts onto ancient scripture, he creates a web of pseudo-miracles that fail under scrutiny.

These attempts at manufacturing miracles demonstrate intellectual dishonesty, undermining both the credibility of the Qur'anic text and the arguments of its defenders. Honest engagement with science and scripture requires acknowledging their differences, rather than fabricating connections that do not exist.

Simplified Rewrite:

Where in the Qur'an is the scientific idea of the Earth's crust floating on a liquid explicitly stated or even implied? The Qur'an's author does not explain why mountains supposedly function as pegs, leaving the concept open to speculation. For example, Islamic scholar Ibn Kathir suggested that mountains prevent the Earth from shaking due to the presence of water beneath it, not because the Earth's crust floats on a liquid layer:

(And has set on the earth firm mountains) means, the mountains stabilize and add weight to the earth, lest it should shake with its water. Allah says: (lest it should shake with you.) (Source: tafsir.com)

Taslaman goes on to cite scientific facts:

"Mountains result from collisions between layers of the Earth's crust. These layers go deeper into the Earth, allowing the crust to integrate and stabilize."

However, where does the Qur'an provide this information? It seems likely that the Qur'an's author was unaware of how mountains form. Unlike modern scientific understanding, the Qur'an consistently portrays mountains as external structures added to the Earth after its creation. This view is why the text describes mountains as being "cast" onto the Earth, similar to rivers and roads. In essence, the Qur'an presents the Earth as being flat and later adorned with mountains, rivers, and pathways:

- *"And He cast on the earth firm mountains, lest it shake with you, and rivers and ways; so happy you will be guided." (Surah 16:15, Arberry)*
- *"And We set mountains on the earth lest it should move with them, and We made on it broad passages between them as routes for their guidance." (Surah 21:31, Rodwell)*
- *"He created the heavens without pillars that you can see, and He threw upon the earth firm mountains lest it should move with you; and He dispersed thereon every sort of beast; and We send down from the heavens water, and We caused to grow therein every noble kind." (Surah 31:10, Palmer)*

The rebuttal above focuses on interpreting the Qur'an properly, showing that its descriptions of mountains do not align with modern geology. Andrew Vargo, in his article *Are Mountains "Pegs" Which Prevent the Earth from Shaking?*, highlights how some Muslim propagandists distort scientific sources to support their claims of miracles.

Special thanks to Jochen Katz (Answering Islam author) for contributing to this article.

Appendix: Harun Yahya's Interpretation of Surah 27:88

In his commentary on Surah 27:88, well-known "miracle hunter" Harun Yahya introduces a new layer to the established pseudo-miracle narrative by adding a fresh claim:

You will see the mountains and reckon them to be solid; but they go past like clouds—the handiwork of Allah Who gives to everything its solidity. He is aware of what you do. (Qur'an, 27:88)

Harun Yahya argues that this verse not only reveals the Earth's rotation but also discloses its direction of movement. He suggests that the comparison of mountain motion to clouds indicates a west-to-east rotation of the Earth. Yahya states:

The direction of movement of the main cloud masses at 3,500-4,000 meters high is always from West to East. That is why it is generally the state of the weather in the West which is looked at in meteorological forecasts. (Source: miraclesofthequran.com)

However, Yahya's assertion is unfounded for several reasons. The verse neither mentions the word "direction" nor explains the direction in which clouds move. The scientific understanding of the Earth's rotation and its direction has been established through extensive studies, not through the Qur'an. Modern Islamic propagandists, including Yahya, are often exposed for distorting scientific facts to fabricate miracles in the Qur'an. Their claims crumble under scrutiny when contrasted with the actual text and scientific evidence.

Scientific and Logical Issues

Yahya's claim is not only unrelated to the Qur'an but also scientifically baseless. Jochen Katz thoroughly debunks the scientific flaws in Yahya's arguments in his article *Harun Yahya's "Science" Fiction – Part 2* (referenced in Chapter VIII of this book). Yahya's approach exemplifies a broader pattern of pseudo-scientific claims propagated by modern Islamic writers.

Footnotes

1. Published in 1989 by *Ankara Diyanet Vakfi* (Foundation for Religion).
2. Halûk Nurbaki, an oncologist, is often compared to Maurice Bucaille for his attempts to link the Qur'an with science.
3. Nurbaki's claims contradict one another. For example, his interpretation of mountains as pegs stabilizing the Earth (pp. 224-226) clashes with his claim that mountains are in constant motion, like clouds. This contradiction undermines both of his pseudo-miracles.
4. Special thanks to Jochen Katz for identifying and clarifying Nurbaki's false analogies.
5. Harun Yahya has also claimed that Surah 27:88 reveals both the Earth's rotation and its direction. This claim is further explored in this appendix.
6. The term *"Qur'an Science Group"* may simply be a grandiose pseudonym for Caner Taslaman.
7. Yahya's miracle claim about the Earth's rotation can also be found on page 109 of his book.
8. These claims are based not on the Qur'anic text itself but on modern scientific advancements. The "miracles" are retroactively imposed onto the text, relying on desperate attempts to align contemporary science with vague Qur'anic verses.
9. The Qur'anic teaching that mountains function as pegs to stabilize the Earth is a scientific error. For further details, see Dr. Campbell's analysis on this topic.

CHAPTER 8

Jonah's contradictions in the Quran

Harun Yahya's "Science" Fiction – Part 2: Misinterpreting Science and the Qur'an

This second installment in my series critiques Harun Yahya's frequent claims of so-called scientific miracles in the Qur'an. As discussed in Chapter VII, a legitimate claim of a scientific miracle in the Qur'an requires three components:

1. A proper interpretation of a Qur'anic verse.
2. A scientifically accurate explanation of the phenomenon in question.
3. A valid connection between the Qur'anic verse and the scientific fact.

Failure in any of these areas invalidates the claim. In this piece, I will expose the failings—or in some cases, deliberate distortions—found in Yahya's approach, particularly regarding his assertion about the Earth's rotation. This particular "miracle" is exceptionally flawed as it fails on all three fronts: the Qur'an is misinterpreted, scientific facts are misrepresented, and the supposed link between the two is unsupported.

Claim: The Qur'an Reveals the Earth's Direction of Rotation

Harun Yahya claims the following verse in the Qur'an reveals not only the Earth's rotation but also its direction:

You will see the mountains and reckon them to be solid; but they go past like clouds—the handiwork of Allah Who gives to everything its solidity. He is aware of what you do. (Qur'an, 27:88)

According to Yahya:

The above verse emphasizes that the Earth not only rotates but that it also has a direction of rotation. The direction of movement of the main cloud masses at 3,500-4,000 meters high is always from West to East. That is why it is generally the state of the weather in the West which is looked at in meteorological forecasts.

Yahya further states:

The main reason why cloud masses are pulled from West to East is the direction in which the Earth rotates. As we now know, our Earth spins from West to East. This scientific fact, only recently established by science, was revealed 1,400 years ago in the Qur'an, at a time when the Earth was believed to be flat and resting on the back of an ox. (Source: miraclesofthequran.com)

Yahya includes the following footnote to support his claims:

"Effects of Rotation (Coriolis Effect)," The Woodrow Wilson National Fellowship Foundation, *www.woodrow.org/teachers/esi/1998/p/weather/Corriolis.HTM.*

Ironically, the very article Yahya references contains information that refutes almost all of his claims. We will explore this in greater depth shortly.

Analysis of Yahya's Claims

1. Misinterpretation of the Qur'an

Harun Yahya's interpretation of Surah 27:88 is a textbook example of distorting scripture. This verse is not about the present time or the Earth's rotation but rather about the Day of Judgment when God will demonstrate His power by making the mountains disappear.

Masud Masihiyyen thoroughly analyzes this verse in *Islamic Dishonesty at Work!* He highlights how Yahya, along with other Muslim propagandists like Halûk Nurbaki and Caner Taslaman, manipulates the text. The verse in its immediate and broader context clearly refers to the end times, not the Earth's rotation. Readers seeking a detailed exegesis of Surah 27:88 are encouraged to consult Masihiyyen's work.

2. Misrepresentation of Science

While some other propagandists attempt to construct a bridge between the Qur'anic text and the idea of Earth's rotation, Yahya skips this step entirely. He merely quotes the verse and makes a bold, unsupported assertion:

The above verse emphasizes that the Earth not only rotates but that it also has a direction of rotation.

This claim is unfounded, as the verse does not include the words *"Earth,"* *"rotation,"* or *"direction."* It does not even hint at Earth's rotation, let alone emphasize it. Moreover, Yahya's attempt to treat direction as an "additional" feature is flawed. Every rotation inherently has a direction; this is not a unique or miraculous revelation.

3. Misunderstanding Cloud Movement and the Coriolis Effect

Yahya's primary argument hinges on the movement of clouds, but his explanation is riddled with scientific inaccuracies. While he references the Coriolis Effect, which explains the deflection of wind and ocean currents due to Earth's rotation, he fails to understand—or deliberately misrepresents—its implications. A detailed reading of the source he cites reveals that the movement of clouds from West to East is a result of atmospheric dynamics, not a direct revelation of Earth's rotation in the Qur'an.

Conclusion

Harun Yahya's claim about the Earth's direction of rotation being revealed in the Qur'an is a prime example of pseudo-science masquerading as divine insight. It fails at every level—misinterpreting the Qur'anic verse, distorting scientific facts, and presenting an unsupported connection between the two. His reliance on misrepresented sources only further undermines his credibility.

This pseudo-miracle demonstrates the broader issue with such claims: they rely on selective interpretations, scientific ignorance, and deliberate manipulation to present a façade of divine knowledge. True science and honest exegesis, however, expose these fabrications for what they are.

Misunderstanding Winds and Cloud Movement: A Rebuttal to Harun Yahya

Harun Yahya claims:

The direction of movement of the main cloud masses at 3,500-4,000 meters high is always from West to East. That is why it is generally the state of the weather in the West which is looked at in meteorological forecasts.
The main reason why cloud masses are pulled from West to East is the direction in which the Earth rotates. As we now know, our Earth spins from West to East.

These statements are riddled with inaccuracies and logical flaws, requiring careful unpacking to address the confusion and misrepresentation of facts.

---

1. Cloud Movement Is Driven by Winds, Not Earth's Rotation

The primary driver of cloud movement is wind, which results from atmospheric pressure differences. While Earth's rotation influences wind patterns through the **Coriolis effect**, this is only one of several factors, including temperature gradients, pressure systems, and topography. Harun Yahya falsely claims that the rotation of the Earth directly determines the direction of cloud movement.

---

2. Cloud Direction Is Not Uniform Across the Globe

Contrary to Yahya's claim, the direction of clouds is not universally west-to-east. Winds, and thus clouds, move in various directions depending on geographical location and weather conditions. While westerly winds are dominant in certain regions, particularly in mid-latitudes (e.g., much of Europe and North America), even in these areas, wind direction can vary significantly.

For instance:

- In Turkey, Yahya's home country, westerly winds are common but not universal. Winds can blow from any direction depending on local weather systems.
- A snapshot of satellite imagery from Turkey during the research for this rebuttal showed clouds moving predominantly south-to-north (SSW to NNE). Over Russia, some clouds were even moving east-to-west in a circular arc.

These observations debunk Yahya's assertion that clouds *"always"* move west-to-east, as this is simply not true.

---

3. No Scientific Basis for the 3,500–4,000 Meter Claim

Yahya's claim that *"main cloud masses at 3,500–4,000 meters high always move from west to east"* is both unsubstantiated and illogical. He provides no references or evidence to support this specific height range.

If the Earth's rotation were indeed the direct cause of cloud movement, it would affect clouds at all altitudes, not just those between 3,500 and 4,000 meters. This arbitrary restriction undermines his argument, exposing it as an attempt to sound scientific while making baseless assertions.

---

4. Internal Contradictions in Yahya's Argument

Ironically, if Yahya's assertion about cloud movement being limited to this height range were true, it would contradict his claim that the

Earth's rotation is the primary cause of cloud movement. Why would the Earth's rotation selectively influence clouds at 3,500–4,000 meters but not those at 2,000 or 5,000 meters? This inconsistency highlights the lack of coherence in his argument.

5. Winds and Their Patterns

Cloud movement is driven by prevailing wind patterns, which differ across the globe due to the Earth's rotation, land-sea distribution, and other atmospheric dynamics. These patterns include:

- **Trade Winds**: Easterly winds in the tropics.
- **Westerlies**: Winds in mid-latitudes that predominantly blow west-to-east.
- **Polar Easterlies**: Easterly winds near the poles.

A detailed wind map (e.g., from Wikipedia or meteorological sources) illustrates the complexity and variability of these wind patterns, further disproving Yahya's simplistic and incorrect claim.

Conclusion

Harun Yahya's statements about cloud movement and the Earth's rotation are scientifically inaccurate and logically flawed. His assertion that clouds *"always"* move west-to-east is demonstrably false, as wind directions vary widely based on geographical and meteorological conditions. Furthermore, his unsubstantiated claim about cloud movement at specific altitudes lacks any scientific grounding and contradicts his argument that the Earth's rotation drives cloud motion.

This analysis reveals Yahya's tendency to misuse scientific concepts in an attempt to align them with Qur'anic verses, ultimately distorting both science and scripture.

Misrepresentation of Cloud Movements and Heights: Rebutting Harun Yahya

While it is true that Turkey lies in a mid-latitude region where westerly winds are common, Harun Yahya's claim that clouds always move from west to east is plainly incorrect when applied to the entire Earth.

Variability in Cloud Movement

Cloud movements are influenced by wind directions, which vary based on atmospheric conditions. At times, even clouds at different heights can move in completely opposite directions. This phenomenon highlights the complexity of wind patterns and undermines Yahya's simplistic assertion about the Earth's rotation determining cloud direction. For example:

- Tornado-associated clouds often exhibit rapid circular motion. How would Yahya reconcile such localized, chaotic patterns with his theory of west-to-east movement?

Cloud Heights: A Misguided Claim

Yahya's arbitrary focus on a cloud height range of 3,500–4,000 meters is unfounded. Clouds appear across a vast range of altitudes, as described in the **Wikipedia article on "Clouds"**:

- **High Clouds (Family A):** Form between 3,000–8,000 m in polar regions, 5,000–12,000 m in temperate zones, and 6,000–18,000 m in tropical regions.
- **Middle Clouds (Family B):** Found between 2,000 m and up to 8,000 m, depending on the region.

- **Low Clouds (Family C):** Located from the surface up to 2,000 m.
- **Moderate Vertical Clouds (Family D1):** Bases range from the surface to about 3,000 m, extending vertically into middle altitudes.
- **Towering Vertical Clouds (Family D2):** These rise dramatically, with bases near the surface or in lower-middle altitudes, extending as high as 10,000 m or more.

Additionally, rarer types of clouds such as **nacreous clouds** form in the stratosphere (15,000–25,000 m), and **noctilucent clouds** appear in the mesosphere at altitudes of 80–85 km.

The Flawed Focus on 3,500–4,000 Meters

Yahya's insistence on this specific height range is both arbitrary and baseless:

- Clouds exist across a wide altitude range, from near the surface to 20,000 meters in tropical regions.
- There is no scientific evidence to suggest that clouds between 3,500–4,000 meters are "main cloud masses" or exhibit unique movement patterns. Yahya offers no data to justify why he chose this narrow range, nor why clouds in this band would always move west-to-east.

Cloud Movement in Towering Clouds

The Wikipedia article also includes an illustrative image of a towering vertical cloud. In its mature stage, such clouds span from about 1,500 to 14,000 meters in altitude. This broad vertical range demonstrates that clouds do not confine themselves to a limited height band as Yahya implies. These towering clouds further challenge his claim, as they are driven by powerful vertical currents and are not influenced solely by Earth's rotation.

Conclusion

Clouds are highly dynamic and are influenced by numerous atmospheric factors beyond Earth's rotation. Harun Yahya's claim that clouds always move west-to-east at a specific altitude of 3,500–4,000 meters is factually incorrect and unsubstantiated. Clouds occur across a vast range of altitudes, and their movements vary widely depending on wind patterns and local weather conditions. Yahya's assertion lacks any scientific basis and fails to account for the complexity of atmospheric dynamics.

Analyzing Harun Yahya's Claims on Cloud Movement and Earth's Rotation

Harun Yahya makes the peculiar claim that clouds at an altitude of **3,500–4,000 meters** always move from **west to east**, asserting this as evidence of a Qur'anic miracle. Let's evaluate his reasoning and expose its flaws.

Selective Claim Without Basis

Yahya provides no credible scientific evidence to justify his narrow focus on clouds at **3,500–4,000 meters** while ignoring the movement of clouds at other altitudes. This selective framing raises serious doubts about his credibility. Unless Yahya can cite a reliable source supporting his statement that "[t]he direction of movement of the main cloud masses at 3,500–4,000 meters high is always from West to East," this claim must be regarded as a fabrication.

Clouds and Earth's Rotation

Cloud movement is determined by wind patterns, not by the Earth's rotation. While the Earth's rotation indirectly influences wind directions (via the **Coriolis effect**), this is just one of many factors. Yahya's claim that clouds **"always"** move west to east is demonstrably false:

- Winds vary by location, altitude, and weather systems, and their directions are not constant.
- Even in regions like Turkey, where **westerly winds** are common, clouds do not always move west to east.

For instance:

- Clouds at different altitudes often move in opposite directions.
- Tornado-associated clouds can rotate in circular patterns, clearly contradicting Yahya's oversimplified assertion.

Cloud Heights: Misleading Focus

Clouds exist at various altitudes, categorized into families:

1. **High Clouds:** 3,000–18,000 meters, depending on the region.
2. **Middle Clouds:** 2,000–8,000 meters.
3. **Low Clouds:** Near surface to 2,000 meters.
4. **Towering Vertical Clouds:** Up to 14,000 meters or more.

The claim that **"main cloud masses"** exist specifically at 3,500–4,000 meters is unsupported. Clouds span a vast range of altitudes, and their movement is dictated by complex atmospheric dynamics—not the Earth's rotation.

Misrepresentation of Sources

Yahya attempts to validate his claims by referencing a scientific paper. However, the **Woodrow Wilson Fellowship Foundation** article he cites directly contradicts his assertions. The article explains:

- Winds in **mid-latitudes** generally blow west to east due to the **Coriolis effect**.
- In the **tropics**, winds blow **east to west**, opposing the Earth's rotation.
- Local weather systems, such as high- and low-pressure areas, often cause winds to blow in various directions.

By misquoting and selectively extracting sentences from the article, Yahya misrepresents its content to fabricate support for his argument. This constitutes intellectual dishonesty.

Scientific Errors

Yahya claims that clouds move west to east because of the Earth's rotation. However:

- If Earth's rotation were the sole cause, all clouds would move uniformly, which they do not.
- Clouds often move **faster** than the Earth's rotation. This additional velocity must be attributed to wind patterns, not the Earth's spin.
- Even if clouds moved solely due to the Earth's rotation, Yahya's specific focus on 3,500–4,000 meters remains inexplicable and baseless.

Closing Remarks

Yahya concludes by asserting:

"As we now know, our Earth spins from West to East. This scientific fact, only recently established by science, was revealed 1,400 years ago in the Qur'an, at a time when the Earth was believed to be flat and resting on the back of an ox."

This statement is riddled with inaccuracies:

1. The Earth's rotation was known long before Islam, as evidenced by **Greek astronomy**.
2. The Qur'an does not explicitly or implicitly mention Earth's rotation. On the contrary, it often reflects a **flat-earth cosmology**, consistent with prevailing beliefs at the time.
3. The notion of Earth resting on an ox is rooted in **Islamic traditions**, not external misconceptions.

Conclusion

Harun Yahya's claims lack scientific and textual support. His misrepresentation of sources and selective focus on unsubstantiated assertions demonstrate intellectual dishonesty. Instead of providing evidence for a Qur'anic miracle, Yahya exposes his own ignorance of both science and historical context, further undermining his credibility.

Ancient Knowledge of Earth's Rotation and Sphericity: A Rebuttal to Harun Yahya

Harun Yahya's claims about the Qur'an revealing the Earth's rotation are not only scientifically flawed but also display a glaring ignorance of historical advancements in astronomy and geography. Here's a summary of ancient knowledge that refutes his assertions.

The Concept of a Spherical Earth

The understanding that the Earth is spherical dates back to ancient Greek philosophy around the **6th century BC**. It became a well-established scientific fact by the **3rd century BC**, thanks to the advancements of Hellenistic astronomy. According to **Wikipedia**:

"The concept of a spherical Earth dates back to ancient Greek philosophy from around the 6th century BC, but remained a matter of philosophical speculation until the 3rd century BC when Hellenistic astronomy established the spherical shape of the earth as a physical given."
(*Wikipedia, "Spherical Earth," accessed on 24 August 2011.*)

Early Philosophers and Earth's Rotation

1. **Hicetas** (c. 400–335 BC), a Greek philosopher of the Pythagorean School, proposed that the daily movement of stars was due to the **Earth's rotation on its axis**.

2. **Heraclides Ponticus** (c. 390–310 BC) also argued that the Earth rotates from west to east once every 24 hours. (*Wikipedia, "Hicetas" and "Heraclides Ponticus," accessed on 24 August 2011.*)

Ironically, Heraclides lived nearly **950 years before the Qur'an** and taught in an area that is now part of Turkey—Harun Yahya's home country. Yet Yahya seems unaware of the scientific history associated with his own region.

Eratosthenes and Precise Measurements

The contributions of **Eratosthenes of Cyrene** (c. 276–195 BC) are particularly noteworthy. He:

- **Calculated the Earth's circumference** with remarkable accuracy using a system of "stades" (stadiums).
- **Determined the tilt of the Earth's axis**.
- Introduced the concepts of **latitude and longitude**. (*Wikipedia, "Eratosthenes," accessed on 24 August 2011.*)

Eratosthenes lived some **800 years before the Qur'an** was revealed. His work provides irrefutable evidence that the concept of a rotating and spherical Earth was well established long before Islamic teachings.

Aryabhata: An Indian Perspective

The Indian mathematician and astronomer **Aryabhata** (476–550 AD), in his magnum opus *Aryabhatiya* (written in 499 AD), explicitly stated that the Earth rotates on its axis. While Aryabhata's works may not have been known in Arabia during Muhammad's time, they demonstrate that ancient scholars independently concluded the Earth's rotation simply by observing their surroundings.

No Divine Revelation, Only Human Observation

The discoveries of Hellenistic and Indian scholars were based on logical reasoning and empirical observation—not divine revelation. These findings are explicit and clear, in stark contrast to the ambiguous language of the Qur'an. Harun Yahya and other propagandists must "read into the text" claims about Earth's rotation because the Qur'an does not explicitly state it.

Misrepresentation of Historical Context

Yahya's ignorance of ancient scientific advancements is evident in his reliance on pseudo-miracle claims. The **flat-earth cosmology** prevalent in early Islamic traditions further undermines his assertions. Ancient Greek astronomers, such as Aristarchus of Samos (310–230 BC), even posited that the Earth revolved around the Sun and rotated on its axis. Yahya's claims are embarrassingly inconsistent with this historical reality. (*Wikipedia, "Aristarchus of Samos," accessed on 24 August 2011.*)

Conclusion

Harun Yahya's argument that the Qur'an revealed the Earth's rotation is baseless. Ancient philosophers and astronomers, living centuries before Muhammad, had already proposed and demonstrated these concepts. The Qur'an offers no clear statement about Earth's rotation, and claims of scientific miracles require substantial distortion of its text.

Yahya's assertions reflect a broader problem in pseudo-miracle apologetics: a deliberate disregard for historical knowledge and scientific accuracy. These claims rely on selective readings and misinterpretations rather than genuine evidence.

CHAPTER 9

The Concept of the Seven Earths

Their Existence and Location

It might surprise some readers to learn that the Qur'an mentions the creation of "seven earths":

"It is Allah Who has created seven heavens, and earths as many..." (Surah 65:12, F. Malik's translation)

This statement raises questions about what these "seven earths" refer to. Are they landmasses, such as the seven continents on our planet? Or do they signify other planets similar to Earth? To evaluate the scientific validity of this claim, we must first understand how this concept was interpreted historically, particularly during Muhammad's time. Insights from early Islamic texts, including *ahadith* (sayings of the Prophet) and Qur'anic commentaries, provide essential context.

Evidence from the Ahadith

Sahih Al-Bukhari

Narrated Muhammad bin Ibrahim bin Al-Harith:

Abu Salama bin 'Abdur-Rahman had a dispute with some people over a piece of land and went to Aisha (the Prophet's wife) for guidance. She said, "O Abu Salama, avoid the land, for Allah's Apostle said: 'Anyone who takes even a span of land unjustly will have it encircled around his neck down through seven earths.'" (Volume 4, Book 54, Number 417; also in Numbers 418, 420; Volume 3, Book 43, Numbers 632-634)

Narrated 'Abdullah:

A Jewish Rabbi came to Allah's Apostle and said, "O Muhammad! We learn that Allah will put all the heavens on one finger, the earths on one finger, and so forth, and then say, 'I am the King.'" Upon hearing this, the Prophet smiled so broadly that his pre-molars became visible, affirming the Rabbi's statement. The Prophet then recited: "No just estimate have they made of Allah such as due to Him." (Surah 39:67) (Volume 6, Book 60, Number 335)

Sahih Muslim

Muhammad b. Ibrahim reported that Abu Salama mentioned a land dispute to Aisha. She warned him, quoting the Prophet:

"Whoever usurps even a span of land will have it wrapped around his neck through seven earths." (Book 10, Number 3925; also in Numbers 3920-3924)

Al-Tirmidhi

Narrated Abu Hurayrah:

The Prophet described the structure of the universe while sitting with his companions. He asked, *"Do you know what these clouds are?"* When they replied, *"Allah and His Messenger know best,"* he explained:

"These are the clouds, the water-carriers of the Earth, driven by Allah to people who neither thank Him nor call upon Him."

He continued with a series of questions:

1. **Above You:**
   - "It is the firmament, a guarded ceiling."
   - "Between you and it are 500 years."
2. **Above That:**
   - Seven heavens are stacked, each separated by a journey of 500 years. Above the seventh heaven lies Allah's Throne.
3. **Below You:**
   - "Underneath you is the Earth."
   - Beneath each earth, there is another, with a journey of 500 years between each.

The Prophet concluded:

"By Him in Whose hand Muhammad's soul is, if you were to drop a rope to the lowest earth, it would not escape Allah's knowledge." He then recited: *"He is the First and the Last, the Outward and the Inward, and He is omniscient."* (Transmitted by Ahmad and Tirmidhi, Number 1513, ALIM CD-ROM Version)

Significance of These Ahadith

This hadith is particularly significant as it does not merely reference the "seven earths" in passing. Here, Muhammad actively teaches his followers about the structure of the universe, describing the relative positions and distances between the seven heavens and seven earths.

Scientific Interpretation

The Qur'an's reference to "seven earths" invites speculation:

1. Are they geographical divisions of our planet, such as continents?
2. Could they represent other planets in the cosmos?

However, the *ahadith* clearly depict a hierarchical cosmology, with the earths stacked below each other, separated by immense distances. This cosmological model does not align with modern scientific understanding of planetary systems or the Earth's structure.

The descriptions also suggest a geocentric worldview prevalent in the 7th century, with little consideration for the scientific discoveries about the Earth's spherical shape or the nature of the universe. Thus, the concept of "seven earths" reflects the beliefs and knowledge of the time rather than a scientifically accurate understanding of the cosmos.

Narrations on the Seven Earths: Existence and Location

Narrated by Ubayy ibn Ka'b:

Regarding the verse from the Qur'an, *"Your Lord brought forth their offspring from the loins of the children of Adam"* (Surah 7:172), Ubayy ibn Ka'b explained:

Allah gathered the offspring of Adam, paired them, and gave them speech, allowing them to testify. He made a covenant with them, asking, *"Am I not your Lord?"* They replied, *"Yes."* Allah then declared, *"I call to witness the seven heavens and the seven earths regarding you ..."* (Transmitted by Ahmad, Number 41 - ALIM CD-ROM Version)

Narrated by Abu Sa'id al-Khudri:

The Prophet (peace be upon him) said:

Moses asked his Lord to teach him something unique to remember and supplicate Him with. Allah instructed him to say, *"There is no god but Allah."* Moses responded that all of Allah's servants already say this and sought something distinctive for himself. Allah replied: *"Moses, if the seven heavens and their inhabitants, apart from Me, and the seven earths were placed on one side of a scale and 'There is no god but Allah' on the other, 'There is no god but Allah' would outweigh them."* (Transmitted in *Sharh as-Sunnah*, Number 731 - ALIM CD-ROM Version)

Narrated by Ya'la ibn Murrah:

The Prophet (peace be upon him) said:

"If anyone wrongfully takes even a span of land, Allah, the Great and Glorious, will make him dig through it to the seventh earth, and it will be tied around his neck on the Day of Resurrection." (Transmitted by Ahmad, Number 885 - ALIM CD-ROM Version)

Prophetic Supplications Involving the Seven Earths

Fiqh-us-Sunna:

Ata ibn Abi Marwan narrates from his father that Ka'b, swearing by the One who parted the sea for Moses, reported:

Whenever the Prophet (peace be upon him) approached a city he intended to enter, he would say: *"O Allah, Lord of the seven heavens and all they shade, Lord of the seven earths and all they carry, Lord of the devils and all they mislead, Lord of the winds and all they scatter, I ask You for the good of this city and its people, and for the good within it. I seek refuge in You from its evil, the evil of its people, and the evil within it."* (Related by an-Nasa'i, Ibn Hibban, and al-Hakim, who deemed it authentic - Volume 2, Number 119b - ALIM CD-ROM Version)

Khalid ibn Walid's Supplication:

Khalid ibn Walid reported suffering from insomnia. The Prophet (peace be upon him) said:

"Shall I teach you some words that will help you sleep? Say: 'O Allah, Lord of the seven heavens and all they cover, Lord of the earths and all they contain, Creator of devils and those they mislead, protect me from the evil of Your creatures lest they harm or transgress against me. Blessed is Your name, and there is no god but You.'" (Reported by At-Tabarani in *Al-Kabir* and *Al-Awsat*, authenticated by Al-Hafiz al-Mundhari - Volume 4, Number 122 - ALIM CD-ROM Version)

Explanations from Early Islamic Scholars and Historians

Tafsir Ibn Abbas:

Regarding Surah 65:12:

"Allah has created seven heavens one above the other like a dome and seven earths beneath them that are flat." "He sends angels with revelations, scriptures, and decrees to the heavens and earth to demonstrate that Allah has power over all things and that His knowledge encompasses everything." (Source: *Tanwîr al-Miqbâs min Tafsîr Ibn 'Abbâs* - altafsir.com)

Al-Tabari:

Muhammad b. Sahl b. Askar narrated from Wahb:

The heavens, earth, and oceans are encompassed by the *haykal* (a structure surrounding the universe). The *haykal* rests upon the Footstool (*Kursi*), with God's feet upon it. Wahb described the *haykal* as a framework encircling the earth and oceans like ropes fastening a tent.

Regarding the earths, Wahb explained: *"There are seven earths, flat and comprising islands. Between each pair of earths lies an ocean. The surrounding ocean encircles all of them, with the haykal behind the ocean."*

(Source: *History of Al-Tabari*, Volume 1, trans. Franz Rosenthal [State University of New York Press, Albany 1989], pp. 207-208)

Conclusion

These narrations and interpretations reveal how early Islamic thought conceptualized the "seven earths." They were understood not as separate planets but as flat, layered realms beneath our own earth. This belief, drawn from prophetic sayings and early commentaries, illustrates a cosmological view that differs significantly from modern scientific understanding.

Ibn Kathir on the Seven Earths

Regarding the verse: *"And of the earth the like thereof"* (Surah 65:12), Ibn Kathir explains:

This means Allah created seven earths. In *Sahih al-Bukhari* and *Sahih Muslim*, there is a hadith that confirms this. At the beginning of my book *Al-Bidayah wan-Nihayah*, I discussed various narrations about the creation of the earth. Praise and thanks be to Allah. Those who interpret this hadith to refer to seven continents offer an explanation that contradicts both the text of the Qur'an and the hadith. Such interpretations lack any supporting evidence. (*Tafsir Ibn Kathir (Abridged)*, Volume 10, Darussalam Publishers, 2000, pp. 55-56)

Muhammad ibn 'Abd Allah al-Kisa'i on the Seven Earths

Muhammad ibn 'Abd Allah al-Kisa'i offers a detailed description of the seven earths:

1. **Ramaka**: Beneath this earth is the *Barren Wind*, restrained by seventy thousand angels. This wind destroyed the people of 'Ad. The inhabitants of Ramaka, called *Muwashshim*, face eternal torment.

2. **Khalada**: Here lie the tools of punishment for Hell's inhabitants. The nation of *Tamis*, dwelling here, consumes their own flesh and blood.
3. **Arqa**: Inhabited by mule-like eagles with spear-like tails, these tails contain 360 poisonous quills. Even one quill could annihilate the entire universe. The people here, called *Qays*, eat dirt and drink milk.
4. **Haraba**: Home to Hell's serpents, as large as mountains with fangs like palm trees. The inhabitants, named *Jilla*, lack eyes, hands, or feet but possess bat-like wings.
5. **Maltham**: Sulfur stones hang around the necks of sinners, with flames leaping onto their faces. The inhabitants, *Hajla*, are numerous and cannibalistic.
6. **Sijjin**: The records of Hell's inhabitants are kept here. Its people, *Qatat*, are bird-like but worship Allah sincerely.
7. **Ajiba**: The domain of Iblis. Its inhabitants, *Khasum*, are short, black, and lion-like with claws. They are destined to dominate Gog and Magog before their destruction. (*Tales of the Prophets - Qisas al-Anbiya*, trans. Wheeler M. Thackston Jr., 1997, pp. 8-9)

Shaykh Al-Albani on the Seven Earths

Renowned hadith scholar Shaykh Al-Albani, citing the narration:

"When death approached Prophet Nuh (Noah), he advised his son: 'I command you with two things and prohibit you from two things. I command you to say La ilaha illa Allah ('There is none worthy of worship except Allah'). If the seven heavens and the seven earths were placed on one side of a scale and La ilaha illa Allah on the other, the latter would outweigh them." (*Silsilah As-Saheehah*, Number 134)

Al-Albani elaborated:

The seven earths are similar to the seven heavens. Numerous ahadith in *Bukhari* and *Muslim* confirm this. The Qur'an also supports this: *"It is Allah who has created seven heavens and of the earth the like thereof."* This indicates similarity in both number and structure.

He criticized dismissive interpretations influenced by modern science, stating:

We should not reject the words of Allah and His Messenger simply because European scientists lack knowledge of these seven earths. As Allah said: *'Of knowledge, you (mankind) have been given only a little.' (Al-Albani, Ahadeeth of Tawheed, Minhaj-us-Sunnah.com)*

Early Islamic Perspectives on the Seven Earths

Evidence from Early Commentators and Historians

1. **Tafsir Ibn Abbas**:

   Allah created seven heavens as domes and seven earths that are flat. He sends angels down with revelation and decrees. His knowledge encompasses everything. (*Tanwîr al-Miqbâs min Tafsîr Ibn 'Abbâs*)

2. **Al-Tabari**:

   The heavens, earth, and oceans are encased in the *haykal* (a framework). The seven earths are flat and separated by oceans. This structure is surrounded by the encompassing ocean, with the *haykal* encircling it. (*History of Al-Tabari*, Volume 1, trans. Franz Rosenthal, 1989, pp. 207-208)

Conclusion

The Islamic texts and early commentaries firmly establish that the concept of "seven earths" was understood by Muhammad and his companions as literal flat layers beneath our earth, not as continents or separate planets. These descriptions align neither with modern scientific understanding of planetary formation nor with the spherical nature of the Earth. Instead, they reflect the cosmological beliefs of the time. For further insights, refer to discussions on the Earth's shape in Islamic thought.

Simplified Translation:

A key observation about this topic is as follows:

- "It is Allah Who has created seven heavens, and earths as many ..." (F. Malik)
- "Allah it is Who hath created seven heavens, and of the earth the like thereof ..." (Pickthall)
- "Allah is He Who created seven Firmaments and of the earth a similar number ..." (Yusuf Ali)

These translations make it clear that the verse is not primarily focused on the number of heavens and earths. Instead, its main purpose is to emphasize **who the creator of the seven heavens and earths is**. The assumption that there are seven heavens and seven earths is presented as a given, not new information.

This belief did not surprise Muhammad's audience or his contemporaries. In the ahadith cited earlier, Muhammad's mention of "seven heavens and seven earths" aligns with what people of his time already believed. For instance, in one hadith, a Jewish Rabbi speaks to Muhammad about the multiple heavens and earths, indicating this was already a common understanding.

The Qur'an does not aim to introduce a novel cosmological model but rather stresses that **Allah alone is the creator of these heavens and**

earths. The purpose of the verse is to affirm Allah's exclusive power and sovereignty over all creation, countering the polytheistic beliefs held by many Arabs at the time. This is reinforced in the verse's conclusion:

"Allah is He Who created seven Firmaments and of the earth a similar number, through the midst of them (all) descends His Command: that ye may know that Allah has power over all things, and that Allah comprehends all things in (His) Knowledge." (Yusuf Ali)

Conclusion

When we consider the early Islamic texts and evidence, it becomes apparent that the Qur'anic description of the universe as having seven heavens and seven earths is a reflection of the common beliefs and superstitions of Muhammad's era. This concept of seven earths is a significant scientific error and was taught by Muhammad as if it were a fact. It was even included in the Qur'an, further reinforcing its erroneous nature.

This demonstrates that Muhammad was not a true prophet of God, the Qur'an is not divinely inspired, and the Allah of Islam is not the true God.

CHAPTER 10
Islam and the Setting of the Sun

Exploring the Traditional Muslim View of the Sun's Orbit

In a previous discussion, we mentioned that the Qur'an teaches that the sun sets in a muddy spring. In this article, we will delve deeper into this topic by examining interpretations from classical Muslim scholars and addressing some modern Muslim responses that attempt to deny this interpretation.

Preliminary Clarifications

It is important to acknowledge that references to the sun rising or setting do not inherently suggest scientific error. These expressions can be understood as everyday speech or **phenomenological language**—language that describes things as they appear from a human perspective. From the earth's viewpoint, the sun does seem to rise and set. Even today, with all our advanced scientific understanding, we continue to use terms like "sunrise" and "sunset" in our everyday speech and meteorological reports.

However, in the case of the Qur'an, the language appears to go beyond mere phenomenological descriptions. There are specific hints in the Qur'an that suggest the author believed the sun physically rises and sets in specific locations. These are most notably found in **Surah 18:86 and 18:90**, which we will analyze to make our case.

The Key Passages

Not all translations of Surah 18:86 interpret the verse the same way. Some say the sun sets in a "muddy spring," while others translate it as a "black sea." Let's compare:

Shakir Translation: *"Until when he reached **the place where the sun set**, he found it going down into a black sea, and found by it a people. We said: O Zul-Qarnain! Either give them a chastisement or do them a benefit... Until when he reached the land of the rising of the sun, he found it rising on a people to whom We had given no shelter from it."* (Surah 18:86, 90)

Yusuf Ali Translation: *"Until, when he reached **the setting of the sun**, he found it set in a spring of murky water: near it, he found a people. We said: 'O Zul-Qarnain! (You have authority) either to punish them or to treat them with kindness'... Until, when he came to the rising of the sun, he found it rising on a people for whom We had provided no covering protection against the sun."*

Some Islamic sources even mention a variant reading, describing the sun setting in a "warm spring."

The Issue

Notice that these verses do not say the sun **appeared** to set in a spring or sea from Zul-Qarnain's perspective. Rather, they explicitly state that Zul-Qarnain reached the **actual place** where the sun sets and rises.

From a scientific standpoint, this is problematic. The earth is a sphere, and the sun is approximately 150 million kilometers away. The "setting of the sun" is always relative to the horizon and cannot be physically reached. Therefore, describing a person traveling to the sun's setting point goes beyond phenomenological language—it suggests a literal belief in such a location, which does not exist. This reflects a misunderstanding of the natural world, likely influenced by legends and myths.

Supporting Evidence from Islamic Sources

Interestingly, Ibn Ishaq, in his biography of Muhammad (*Sirat Rasulullah*), quotes a poem attributed to Tubba:

Dhu'l-Qarnayn before me was a Muslim,
Conquered kings thronged his court,
East and west he ruled, yet he sought
Knowledge true from a learned sage.
He saw where the sun sinks from view
In a pool of mud and fetid slime.

(Alfred Guillaume, *The Life of Muhammad*, p. 12)

This poem seems to corroborate the Qur'anic depiction of the sun setting in a muddy spring and suggests that Muhammad may have incorporated a pre-Islamic legend into the Qur'an.

A Side Note on the Word "Muslim"

It is worth noting that the term "Muslim" appears in this supposedly pre-Islamic poem. This raises questions about its authenticity. It could indicate that the poem was fabricated by Muslims after Muhammad's time. Alternatively, if the term was genuinely in use before Islam, it would suggest that Muhammad borrowed religious terminology and ideas from existing traditions, assuming them to be divinely revealed concepts.

Conclusion

The Qur'anic description of the sun setting in a muddy spring (or black sea) reflects a misunderstanding of the natural world. The depiction of Zul-Qarnain traveling to the place where the sun sets indicates a literal belief in such a location, which is scientifically incorrect. This aligns with pre-Islamic legends rather than divine revelation, casting doubt on the Qur'an's claim of being a flawless and divinely inspired text.

Islam and the Setting of the Sun:

Exploring Quranic Descriptions of the Sun's Movement

The Qur'an references the setting and rising of the sun in various places, including the story of Ibrahim (Abraham):

"Thus did We show Ibrahim the kingdom of the heavens and the earth, that he might be of those who are sure. When the night overshadowed him, he saw a star and said, 'Is this my Lord?' But when it set, he said, 'I do not love those that set.' Then, when he saw the moon rising, he said, 'Is this my Lord?' But when it set, he said, 'If my Lord had not guided me, I would certainly have been among the erring people.' Finally, when he saw the sun rising, he said, 'Is this my Lord? This is the greatest.' But when it set, he said, 'O my people, I am free from what you associate with Allah. I have turned my face towards Him Who created the heavens and the earth, as a true believer, and I am not of the polytheists.'" (Surah 6:75–79, Shakir)

It could be argued that this passage reflects Abraham's observations, describing how the sun, moon, and stars appeared to him to rise and set from his vantage point. However, this interpretation raises two significant issues.

1. Comparing with Zul-Qarnain

If Surah 18:86 is also speaking from Zul-Qarnain's perspective—suggesting the sun merely *appeared* to set in a muddy spring—why doesn't the text make this clear? Unlike the story of Abraham, where the Qur'an explicitly describes his observations, the narrative of Zul-Qarnain provides no such clarification. The text states that Zul-Qarnain *reached the place* where the sun sets and rises. This specificity suggests that the Qur'an's author intended to convey a literal understanding, where the sun physically sets in a spring or sea and rises from another location.

2. The Sun's Movement in the Qur'an

The Qur'an repeatedly emphasizes that the sun, moon, and stars travel along set courses, as seen in the following verses:

- *"Have you not considered him (Namrud) who disputed with Ibrahim about his Lord, because Allah had given him the kingdom? When Ibrahim said: 'My Lord is He Who gives life and causes to die,' he said: 'I give life and cause death.' Ibrahim said: 'Surely Allah causes the sun to rise from the East; then make it rise from the West.' Thus, the one who disbelieved was confounded, and Allah does not guide the unjust." (Surah 2:258, Shakir)*
- *"Allah is He Who raised up the heavens without any pillars that you can see. Then He settled Himself on the Throne and pressed the sun and the moon into your service; each planet pursues its course until an appointed term. He regulates all affairs and clearly explains the Signs, so that you may have firm belief in meeting your Lord." (Surah 13:2, Sher Ali)*
- *"And He has made the sun and the moon subservient to you, pursuing their courses, and has made the night and the day subservient to you." (Surah 14:33, Shakir)*
- *"And thou couldst see the sun, as it rose, move away from their Cave on the right, and when it set, turn away from them on the left." (Surah 18:17, Sher Ali)*
- *"Bear patiently what they say, and glorify your Lord with His praise before the rising of the sun and before its setting; and glorify Him in the hours of the night and all parts of the day, that you may find true happiness." (Surah 20:130, Sher Ali)*

- *"And He it is Who created the night and the day, and the sun and the moon. They float, each in an orbit." (Surah 21:33, Pickthall)*
- *"And the sun runs to a resting place for it. That is the decree of the Mighty, the Wise. And the moon, We have measured for it mansions till it returns like an old shriveled palm-leaf. It is not for the sun to overtake the moon, nor does the night outstrip the day. They float, each in an orbit." (Surah 36:38–40, Pickthall)*
- *"He created the heavens and the earth in true proportions. He makes the night overlap the day, and the day overlap the night. He has subjected the sun and the moon; each one follows a course for an appointed time." (Surah 39:5, Yusuf Ali)*

Collective Analysis

When these verses are considered collectively, it becomes clear that the Qur'an describes the sun, moon, and stars as rising and setting while traveling along fixed courses. This suggests that the author of the Qur'an believed in a literal movement of these celestial bodies.

This further implies that Abraham's experience was not simply an observational phenomenon. The Qur'an's author seems to believe that Abraham was witnessing the actual movement of the sun, moon, and stars as they traversed their orbits.

Conclusion

The most straightforward interpretation of Surah 18:86 and 90 is that Zul-Qarnain found the literal setting and rising locations of the sun, as described in the Qur'an. The insistence by some to reinterpret these verses as phenomenological language arises from a desire to reconcile the Qur'an with modern scientific understanding. However, the text itself does not support such reinterpretation. Instead, it reveals a worldview rooted in the cosmological ideas of its time, which are inconsistent with contemporary scientific knowledge.

The Commentators

The interpretation of Surah 18:86 has been a subject of debate among Muslim scholars, primarily due to variant readings of the Quranic text. Some versions state that the sun sets in "murky waters," while others use the term "warm" instead of "murky." These discrepancies highlight the existence of variations in the transmission of the Quran, challenging the traditional Islamic claim of a perfectly preserved text without any alterations or inconsistencies.

The Debate Over "Murky" vs. "Warm"

It is somewhat intriguing to observe how early Muslim scholars and commentators were preoccupied with whether the sun set in a muddy or warm spring. This discussion strongly suggests that the author of the Quran, or at least Muhammad and his contemporaries, believed in the literal setting of the sun in a spring. If the passage were merely describing what Zul-Qarnain *saw*—an optical illusion of the sun setting into a spring—why would the exact nature of the spring (muddy or warm) matter? Whether murky or warm, the description would be irrelevant if the verse were intended as phenomenological language rather than a literal account.

Moreover, a review of the early Islamic commentaries shows that many scholars went to great lengths to deny the literal interpretation that the sun sets in a spring. These efforts reflect an attempt to reconcile the Quranic narrative with a more scientifically acceptable understanding, a topic we will address in detail later.

Tafsir Ibn Abbas

"Till, when he reached the setting place of the sun (where the sun sets), he found it setting in a muddy spring, a blackened, muddy, and stinking spring; it is also said that this means a hot spring, and he found a people thereabout who were disbelievers. We said: 'O Dhu'l-Qarnayn,

either punish them (kill them until they believe in Allah) or show them kindness (pardon them)." (Tanwîr al-Miqbâs min Tafsîr Ibn 'Abbâs, commentary on Surah 18:86; source: altafsir.com)

Ibn Kathir's Commentary

Ibn Kathir interprets the verse as follows:

*""Until, when he reached the setting of the sun' means that Zul-Qarnain traveled until he reached the furthest point west on earth, the westernmost part of the land. Regarding the claim by storytellers that he traveled to the actual place where the sun sets in the sky, this is a baseless myth primarily invented by the People of the Book and their heretical storytellers.

'He found it set in a spring of murky water,' means Zul-Qarnain saw the sun from his perspective as if it descended into the ocean, just as anyone standing on the seashore sees the sun seemingly descending into the horizon. However, in reality, the sun does not leave its orbit in the fourth heaven.

The term 'Hami'a' (murky) comes from the word 'Hama'a', meaning clay, as Allah mentions in the verse, 'I am creating humans from clay' (Surah 15:28). Another variant reading renders the word as 'Hamiya,' meaning warm. Both interpretations are valid, as supported by narrations attributed to Ibn Abbas and Kab Al-Ahbar."*

Ibn Kathir further elaborates with narrations:

- *"The Prophet (peace be upon him) said the sun sets in a warm spring, as narrated by Ali Ibn Abu Talha from Ibn Abbas."*
- *"Kab Al-Ahbar also confirmed the Torah describes the sun setting in mud."*

Ibn Kathir concludes:

"Both readings—'Hami'a'* (muddy) and *'Hamiya'* (warm)—are correct. There is no contradiction, as the spring could be warm and muddy due to exposure to the sun's heat."*

The Historical Debate

Ibn Kathir's and other commentators' explanations demonstrate that early Islamic scholars grappled with reconciling the Quranic text with observable phenomena. They provided various interpretations, ranging from metaphorical explanations to literal accounts, such as the sun setting in physical mud or water.

The fascination with whether the spring was muddy or warm further underscores that early Muslims did not view the description as purely symbolic or phenomenological. Instead, they treated it as a literal account, reflecting the beliefs and cosmological understanding of the time.

Ultimately, this interpretation reveals the challenges faced by Muslim commentators in defending the Quran's descriptions of natural phenomena, particularly in the face of modern scientific knowledge.

Rewritten Text:

Ibn Hadir's Account Ibn Hadir said to Ibn Abbas, "If I had been present earlier with you, I would have shared something to clarify the matter of the warm spring." Ibn Abbas asked, "What would that be?" Ibn Hadir replied, "Regarding the account of Zul-Qarnain, who followed a path of knowledge, he traveled across the earth, both east and west, seeking the reasons for his journey, as commanded by a wise guide. At dusk, he saw the sun DESCENDING INTO a spring described as *Khulb, Thatin,* and *Harmad.*"

Ibn Abbas then inquired, "What does *Khulb* mean?" Ibn Hadir explained, "In their language, it means mud."

164

Ibn Abbas asked, "And what is *Thatin*?" He replied, "It means warmth."

He then asked, "What about *Harmad*?" Ibn Hadir said, "It means black."

Ibn Abbas, impressed by the explanation, requested a male youth to record Ibn Hadir's words, saying, "Write down what this man says."

Sa'id Ibn Jubair narrated that Ibn Abbas recited Surah Al-Kahf (18:86) and read the verse, *"He found it setting in a spring of murky water (Hama'a)."* Kab responded, "By Him who holds my soul in His hand, I have not heard anyone recite it as accurately as Ibn Abbas does, consistent with the way it is revealed in the Torah. In the Torah, it is described as descending into a black clod of mud." *(Source: quran.al-islam.com; translated by Dimitrius)*

Al-Jalalayn Commentary *"Until he reached the place of the setting of the sun"* refers to WHERE THE SUN APPEARS TO SET. *"He found it setting in a spring of murky water (Hama'a)"*—*Hama'a* refers to black mud. The description of the sun setting into a spring is based on the visual perception of the observer, as the sun is far larger than the earth. Zul-Qarnain encountered a tribe living around this spring, who were unbelievers. *(Source: quran.al-islam.com; translated by Dimitrius)*

Al-Tabari's Interpretation The Almighty says: *"Until he reached the place of the setting of the sun, he found it setting in a spring of murky water."* This verse addresses Zul-Qarnain's journey.

Regarding *"the place of the setting of the sun, he found it setting in a spring of murky water"*, there has been disagreement among scholars about the precise reading of the term.

- Some scholars from Medina and Basra recite it as *Hami'a spring*, meaning the sun sets in a spring containing mud.
- A group from Medina and the majority from Kufa read it as *Hamiya spring*, meaning the sun sets in a spring of warm water.

The interpretations differ based on the pronunciation and reading of the term. *(Source: quran.al-islam.com; translated by Dimitrius)*

Addressing Objections

These accounts reveal the variety of interpretations among early Muslim commentators. They grappled with the apparent literal implications of the verse, debating whether the spring was muddy or warm, and sought ways to reconcile these descriptions with their theological perspectives. This discussion sheds light on the challenges of interpreting the Quranic text in a way that aligns with modern understanding and scientific realities.

Rewritten Text:

Refuting Muslim Apologists: MENJ and Hesham Azmy's Claims on the Sun Setting in a Muddy Spring

Muslim apologists MENJ (of the *Bismiikaalahuma* website) and Hesham Azmy have attempted to refute the assertion that the Quran teaches the sun literally sets in a muddy spring. Their arguments, however, have been thoroughly addressed and dismantled. Christian authors M. Rafiqul-Haqq and P. Newton have provided an excellent critique, highlighting the flaws in the typical Muslim explanations. They effectively demonstrate that the Quranic depiction of Zul-Qarnain and the sun setting in a muddy spring is heavily influenced by pre-Islamic myths and legends about Alexander the Great.

This article aims to counter the claims of these Muslim authors by examining their own cited sources, including classical Islamic scholars like Ibn Kathir and al-Qurtubi. While MENJ and Azmy argue that the Quran does not speak of the sun literally setting in a muddy spring, we will show how the same scholars they rely upon inadvertently pose serious challenges to their argument that the Quran is scientifically accurate.

Citing Muslim Scholars

MENJ and Azmy quote the following explanation from al-Qurtubi:

"It is not meant by reaching the rising or setting of the sun that he reached its body and touched it because it runs in the sky around the earth without touching it, and it is too great to enter any spring on earth. It is so much larger than the earth. But it is meant that he reached the end of populated land east and west, so he found it—according to his vision—setting in a spring of murky water, like we watch it in smooth land as if it enters inside the land. That is why He said, 'he found it rising on a people for whom we had provided no covering protection against the sun' (Surah 18:90) and did not mean that it touches or adheres to them; but they are the first to rise on. Probably this spring is a part of the sea, and the sun sets behind, with or at it, so the proposition takes the place of an adjective, and God knows best." (*Translation by Azmy and MENJ; Arabic source: quran.al-islam.com*)

Azmy and MENJ also cite the opinions of ar-Razi and Ibn Kathir. For brevity, we will not re-quote Ibn Kathir here but encourage readers to review his earlier comments, as well as those of al-Jalalayn, which deny that the Quran literally teaches the sun sets in a spring.

Analysis of the Scholars' Denials

The denials by Ibn Kathir, al-Qurtubi, ar-Razi, and al-Jalalayn that the Quran should be taken literally in this case are not based on the text itself. Instead, these interpretations arise from their awareness that the sun is far larger than the earth and cannot literally set in a spring. Much like modern Muslims, these scholars, constrained by their belief in the

Quran's infallibility, sought to reconcile its text with their more advanced understanding of science.

Flaws in the Appeal to Classical Scholars

Relying on these scholars presents a significant problem: both Ibn Kathir and al-Qurtubi espoused erroneous scientific views that they claimed were based on the Quran and hadith. For instance, they asserted that the earth rests on the back of a giant whale, with mountains serving to stabilize it. This view, derived from Islamic traditions, demonstrates the limitations of their scientific understanding. (*See more details here: The Whale and the Earth.*)

Moreover, Ibn Kathir also believed, based on Muhammad's teachings, that the sun physically travels through the seven heavens to prostrate under Allah's throne before returning to its course. Commenting on Surah 36:38, Ibn Kathir wrote:

"There are two views regarding the phrase *'on its fixed course for a term (appointed)'*:

1. It refers to its fixed location beneath the Throne, beyond the earth in that direction. Wherever it moves, it is beneath the Throne, along with all of creation. The Throne is the *roof* of creation, not a sphere as astronomers claim. It is a *dome supported by legs or pillars*, carried by angels, and above the universe. When the sun is at its zenith at noon, it is closest to the Throne; at midnight, when it is at the opposite point, it is furthest away. At that time, the sun prostrates and asks permission to rise again, as stated in the hadiths."

Ibn Kathir then cites a narration from Al-Bukhari:

Abu Dharr reported: "I was with the Prophet in the mosque at sunset, and he said: 'O Abu Dharr! Do you know where the sun sets?' I replied, 'Allah and His Messenger know best.' He said: 'It goes and prostrates beneath the Throne. That is what Allah means when He says: *"And the sun runs on its fixed course for a term. That is the decree of the Almighty, the All-Knowing."""*

This view further underscores the flawed scientific understanding held by classical Islamic scholars, based on their interpretation of the Quran and traditions.

Conclusion

The attempts by MENJ and Azmy to deny the Quran's literal description of the sun setting in a muddy spring fail to address the underlying issues. The very scholars they rely upon to defend their position—such as Ibn Kathir and al-Qurtubi—hold views that conflict with modern scientific knowledge, undermining their arguments. Additionally, these scholars' explanations are based on their belief in the Quran's inerrancy, not on the actual text itself.

This demonstrates that the Quranic description of the sun setting in a muddy spring aligns more with pre-Islamic myths and legends than with established scientific facts.

Rewritten Text:

(**The second view**) suggests that this refers to the sun's appointed end on the Day of Resurrection, when its fixed course will cease. At that time, the sun will come to a halt, and it will be rolled up as this world comes to an end. This marks the termination of its appointed time. This is what is meant by the fixed course of its time... (*Tafsir Ibn Kathir Abridged*, Volume 8: *Surat Al-Ahzab, Verse 51 to the End of Surat Ad-Dukhan*, abridged by a group of scholars under the supervision of Shaykh Safiur-Rahman Al-Mubarakpuri [Darussalam Publishers & Distributors, Riyadh, Houston, New York, London, Lahore; September 2000, first edition], pp. 196-197; bold and capital emphasis ours).

When we combine the Quran's statements with Muhammad's narrations as reported by Ibn Kathir about the sun's course, the conclusion becomes clear: the sun follows a designated path that includes setting in a muddy spring and presenting itself before Allah above the seven heavens. Allah has ordained that the sun must travel this path, which involves setting in a muddy spring and appearing in His presence. For further details, refer to Al-Tabari's traditions cited below.

The preceding comments from Ibn Kathir reveal a troubling pattern. When Muslim scholars encountered Quranic statements that contradicted the scientific knowledge of their time, they quickly sought to reinterpret or explain them away. Yet, when the Quran mentioned phenomena that were unknown from a scientific perspective, these same scholars were eager to affirm that the passages referred to actual scientific facts.

Furthermore, there were times when these commentators opposed the prevailing scientific beliefs of their era because those views clearly contradicted the Quran. However, as modern science has progressed, further research has shown that the scientists of that time were closer to the truth than the Quranic interpretations. This has exposed clear errors in the Quran.

This leaves MENJ and Azmy in a challenging position. If the interpretations and exegesis of scholars like Ibn Kathir are deemed reliable enough to explain passages such as Surah 18:86, then they must also be considered valid when interpreting other Quranic claims, such as the sun's journey or the idea that mountains serve as pegs to stabilize the earth.

To selectively appeal to these commentators—accepting their interpretations in some cases while dismissing them in others—cannot be considered intellectually honest. The appendix will delve further into these texts and the unavoidable conclusions that arise from them.

Rewritten Text:

The 'Space Travel' Interpretation

At least one classical commentator explicitly introduced an alternative idea regarding the location of the spring into which the sun sets. This interpretation attempts to "resolve" the issue that there is no location on earth where the sun literally sets—whether in a muddy spring or any other physical place.

Some Muslim commentators argue that the Quran does not teach that the sun literally sets on the earth. After all, the Quran does not explicitly state that the spring or ocean into which the sun sets is located on earth. Let us revisit the passage in question:

"They will question thee concerning Dhool Karnain. Say: 'I will recite to you a mention of him. We established him in the land, and We gave him a way to everything; and he followed a way until, when he REACHED THE SETTING OF THE SUN, he found IT SETTING IN a muddy spring, and he found NEARBY a people. We said, 'O Dhool Karnain, either thou shalt chastise them, or thou shalt take towards them a way of kindness.' He said, 'As for the evildoer, him we shall chastise, then he shall be returned to his Lord and He shall chastise him with a horrible chastisement. But as for him who believes, and does righteousness, he shall receive as recompense the reward most fair, and we shall speak to him, of our command, easiness.' Then he followed a way until, when he reached the rising of the sun, he found it rising upon a people for whom We had not appointed ANY VEIL TO SHADE THEM FROM IT." (Surah 18:83-89, A.J. Arberry)

We are not disputing that the text describes the sun literally setting in a spring or ocean—it clearly does. The key question is whether this spring or ocean is located on earth. To better explore this idea, let us turn to *Tafsir al-Tabari*, which includes traditions attributed to Muhammad and his companions:

Al-Tabari's Report on the Sun's Setting

Al-Tabari narrates an intriguing tradition:

A man approached Ibn Abbas, saying, *"I heard Ka'b, the Rabbi, tell a remarkable story about the sun and the moon."* Ibn Abbas, who had been reclining, sat up and asked, *"What did he say?"* The man replied, *"He claimed that on the Day of Resurrection, the sun and moon will be brought forth like two hamstrung oxen and thrown into Hell."*

Hearing this, Ibn `Abbas became visibly angry, exclaiming three times, *"Ka'b is lying! Ka'b is lying! Ka'b is lying! This is a Jewish fabrication he is trying to inject into Islam. God is far too majestic to punish servants that are obedient to Him. Have you not read God's words: 'He subjected the sun and the moon, each running for an appointed term'?"*

After refuting Ka'b's claim, Ibn `Abbas recounted what he had heard from Muhammad: *"When God completed creation, He created two suns from the light of His Throne. But foreknowing that He would efface one and turn it into the moon, He created it smaller in size. Yet, both appear small to us because of their altitude and distance from the earth. If He had left them both as suns, night and day would not have been distinguishable, and human life would lack rhythm and order."*

Springs for the Sun's Setting and Rising

Al-Tabari further explains that God created **180 springs in the west made of black clay** where the sun sets and **180 springs in the east** where it rises. These springs bubble and boil like a pot on a furious flame. Each day and night, the sun rises and sets in a new spring. This daily shift results in the changing durations of daylight throughout the year, with the longest days in summer and the shortest in winter.

This is captured in God's words:

"The Lord of the two easts and the Lord of the two wests." (Surah 55:17)

The reference to multiple easts and wests signifies the many positions of the sun as it rises and sets.

Implications of This Interpretation

This interpretation suggests that the Quran's author—based on the traditions preserved by early commentators—believed in a literal setting and rising of the sun in specific springs. Furthermore, the idea of multiple springs, combined with the sun's travel through them, reflects a cosmological understanding rooted in mythological traditions.

This raises serious questions for those who argue that the Quran's statements on the sun's setting are purely allegorical or phenomenological. Instead, the text and its traditional interpretations seem to reflect an attempt to describe the physical universe based on pre-Islamic cosmological ideas.

Rewritten Text:

The 'Space Travel' Version of the Sun's Setting

In one classical commentary, a unique interpretation was introduced regarding the location of the spring into which the sun sets. This interpretation attempts to "resolve" the issue that no such location exists on Earth, whether it be a muddy spring or any other kind of place.

Some Muslim commentators argue that the Quran does not explicitly teach that the sun sets on Earth. After all, the text does not specifically state that the spring or ocean where the sun sets is located on Earth. Let us revisit the passage in question:

"They will question thee concerning Dhool Karnain. Say: 'I will recite to you a mention of him. We established him in the land, and We gave him a way to everything; and he followed a way until, when he REACHED THE SETTING OF THE SUN, he found IT SETTING IN a muddy spring, and he found NEARBY a people. We said, 'O Dhool Karnain, either thou shalt chastise them, or thou shalt take towards them a way of kindness.' He said, 'As for the evildoer, him we shall chastise, then he shall be returned to his Lord and He shall chastise him with a horrible chastisement. But as for him who believes, and does righteousness, he shall receive as recompense the reward most fair, and we shall speak to him, of our command, easiness.' Then he followed a way until, when he reached the rising of the sun, he found it rising upon a people for whom We had not appointed ANY VEIL TO SHADE THEM FROM IT." (Surah 18:83-89, A.J. Arberry)

While the text does clearly describe the sun setting in a spring or ocean, the real question is whether this spring or ocean is on Earth. To explore this idea further, we examine *Tafsir al-Tabari*, which includes traditions attributed to Muhammad and his companions.

Al-Tabari's Report on the Sun's Setting

Al-Tabari recounts a detailed tradition:

Ibn `Abbas narrated that God created an ocean three farsakhs (approximately 18 kilometers) below the heavens. This ocean, held aloft by God's command, stands suspended in the air. Its waves remain contained, and not a single drop is spilled. Unlike all other oceans, which are motionless, this celestial ocean flows as swiftly as an arrow. It stretches like a taut rope across the space between east and west. The sun, the moon, and the retrograde stars *run within its deep swells*. This is what God meant in the Quran when He said: *"Each swims in a sphere."* The "sphere" refers to the sun's circulation within the ocean's currents.

The Prophet Muhammad further elaborated that if the sun were to emerge from this ocean, it would incinerate everything on Earth, including rocks and stones. Similarly, if the moon were to rise from the ocean, its heat would devastate life on Earth, leading people to worship gods other than Allah—except for those Allah protects.

The Retrograde Stars and Their Orbits

When asked about the "retrograde stars" (al-khunnas) mentioned in the Quran, Muhammad identified them as five celestial bodies: Jupiter (al-birjis), Saturn (zuhal), Mercury (`utarid), Mars (bahram), and Venus (al-zuhrah). These stars, like the sun and moon, move and orbit along their appointed paths. All other stars, however, are suspended in the heavens like lamps in a mosque, rotating in unison with the celestial sphere.

Muhammad explained that these heavenly bodies circulate in prayer, glorifying Allah. On the Day of Resurrection, this rotation will become as swift as a millstone's spinning, reflecting the tremors and calamities of that day. The Quranic verse, *"On a day when the heaven sways to and fro and the mountains move,"* refers to this apocalyptic event.

The Sun's Daily Journey

Al-Tabari also narrates that every morning, the sun rises from its chariot in one of the celestial springs, accompanied by 360 angels. These angels, with their wings spread, guide the sun along its path, glorifying Allah throughout the hours of the day and night.

When God wishes to display His power and warn His servants, the sun may fall from its chariot into the depths of the celestial ocean, causing an eclipse. A full solar eclipse occurs when the entire sun falls into the ocean, plunging the world into darkness. A partial eclipse happens when only part of the sun submerges. In either case, angels retrieve the sun, lifting it back to its chariot and resuming its celestial course.

At sunset, the sun is carried westward and *placed into the spring*. This cycle repeats daily, with the sun prostrating beneath Allah's throne each night, as mentioned in the Quran and prophetic traditions.

The Cosmology of the Seven Earths and Oceans

Al-Tabari also discusses the Quranic cosmology, which includes seven earths and seven seas. Each of the seven seas surrounds the one before it, and the final sea is said to be encircled by an immense cosmic structure called the *haykal*. The haykal acts as a boundary for the heavens and earth, with the entire creation resting upon Allah's Footstool.

Al-Tabari further describes the seven seas by name, noting their vastness and unique characteristics. These seas and their inhabitants are said to be sustained by Allah's provision, underscoring His sovereignty over all creation.

Implications of the Narrative

According to these traditions, the ocean in which the sun sets is not located on Earth but in a celestial realm outside the planet. This implies that Zul-Qarnain's journey may have taken him beyond the Earth's atmosphere to encounter otherworldly beings near the setting place of the sun. While this interpretation might sound speculative, it is consistent with the descriptions found in early Islamic traditions.

Al-Tabari's accounts demonstrate that the Quran's cosmology, as understood by early Muslim scholars, was deeply rooted in mythological ideas, blending celestial phenomena with divine orchestration.

Revised Text:

The Seven Earths and Their Inhabitants

According to Islamic tradition, there are seven earths, each with unique characteristics and inhabitants:

1. **Ramaka**: Beneath this earth lies the *Barren Wind*, restrained by no fewer than seventy thousand angels. This wind was used by God to destroy the people of `Ad. The inhabitants of Ramaka are a nation called *Muwashshim*, condemned to everlasting torment and divine punishment.
2. **Khalada**: This earth contains the tools of torture for the residents of Hell. A nation called *Tamis* resides here, feeding on their own flesh and drinking their own blood.
3. **Arqa**: Home to mule-like eagles with tails resembling spears. Each tail has 360 poisonous quills, and even one quill, if placed on the face of the earth, would obliterate the entire universe. The inhabitants, known as *Qays*, survive by eating dirt and drinking mothers' milk.
4. **Haraba**: This earth is inhabited by the serpents of Hell, as massive as mountains, with fangs like towering palm trees. A single strike from these fangs would level even the mightiest mountain. The inhabitants, called *Jilla*, lack eyes, hands, or feet but possess bat-like wings and only die of old age.
5. **Maltham**: Here, sulfur stones hang around the necks of unbelievers. When the fire is ignited, its fuel is placed on their chests, causing flames to engulf their faces, as referenced in the Quran: *"The fire whose fuel is men and stones" (2:24), and "Fire shall cover their faces" (14:50)*. The inhabitants, a nation called *Hajla*, are numerous and cannibalistic.
6. **Sijjin**: This earth holds the records of the wicked, as mentioned in the Quran: *"Verily the register of the actions of the wicked is surely Sijjin" (83:7)*. The inhabitants, called *Qatat*, are bird-like beings who faithfully worship God.

7. **Ajiba**: The dwelling place of Iblis (Satan). It is inhabited by a nation called *Khasum*, described as black, short, and possessing lion-like claws. This nation is prophesied to rule over Gog and Magog and eventually destroy them.

(Source: Muhammad ibn 'Abd Allah al-Kisa'i, Qisas al-Anbiya (Tales of the Prophets), trans. Wheeler M. Thackston Jr., pp. 8-9)

The Supernatural Transport of Zul-Qarnain

Islamic traditions also recount Allah's miraculous transportation of Muhammad during the *Night Journey*, taking him from the Ka'bah to Jerusalem and through the seven heavens: Source. From this perspective, it is conceivable that Zul-Qarnain could have been supernaturally transported to an otherworldly realm—the very location where the sun is said to set—in order to subjugate the inhabitants there.

Myth or Reality?

This does not mean that these stories are factual, such as Muhammad's journey through the seven heavens or Zul-Qarnain's alleged transportation to an extraterrestrial domain. Instead, it underscores how the Quran and hadith literature present fables and myths as if they were facts. This reflects the legendary and mythical nature of the Quran, which records stories steeped in pre-Islamic folklore and cosmological misconceptions.

The narratives also highlight significant scientific inaccuracies and flawed cosmological views held by the Quran's author(s) and the early Muslim community, as noted by scholars like al-Tabari.

Modern science makes it unequivocally clear that the sun does not "set in a muddy spring," whether on earth or elsewhere. The sun does not vanish at night only to reappear in the morning. Instead, it is always shining, visible to half of the earth's surface at any given moment, as our planet rotates on its axis.

A Contradiction?

When we compare the interpretations of al-Tabari and Ibn Kathir, they appear to present conflicting understandings of the location where the sun sets as described in Surah 18:86. Al-Tabari suggests that these springs exist outside of the earth, while Ibn Kathir explicitly states:

"... until he reached the furthest point West that a person can reach **on earth**, which is the **western part of earth**. ... Regarding what was mentioned of Zul-Qarnain following a path with knowledge, he traveled **the earth** both east and west seeking the reasons..."

Clearly, Ibn Kathir speaks of Zul-Qarnain's journey as being confined to the surface of the earth, with no suggestion of space travel.

Reconciling the Contradiction

Al-Tabari's account introduces a unique perspective:

"God created an ocean three farsakhs (18 kilometers) removed from heaven. Waves contained, it stands in the air by the command of God. No drop of it is spilled. All the oceans are motionless, but that ocean flows at the rate of the speed of an arrow... The sun, the moon, and the retrograde stars **run in its deep swell**..."

This suggests that the ocean, where the sun sets, is situated within the first heaven, inside our atmosphere. Al-Tabari specifies that the ocean is merely 18 kilometers from heaven, a relatively small distance. Therefore, one could harmonize the two accounts by suggesting that the "spring" into which the sun sets is located at the edge of the flat earth, near the dome of heaven, but not on the earth itself. In this view,

Zul-Qarnain would have reached and seen the spring without leaving the earth's surface.

This interpretation aligns the two views but simultaneously highlights the Quranic cosmology's inaccuracies. It assumes a flat earth with a defined edge and is entirely inconsistent with modern scientific understanding.

Implications for the Shape of the Earth

Ibn Kathir's interpretation raises further issues:

"… until he reached the furthest point West that a person can reach on earth, which is the western part of earth."

On a spherical earth, there is no absolute east or west. Traveling in either direction indefinitely will bring one back to the starting point. While a flat earth could theoretically have extreme points in all four cardinal directions (north, south, east, west), a spherical earth only has fixed extremes at the poles. Thus, the concept of an "absolute west" or "absolute east" does not exist on a globe.

If these terms are understood relative to a specific geographic point (e.g., Mecca), the furthest points east and west would be identical, located 180 degrees apart in longitude. However, the Quran describes these as two distinct locations reached by Zul-Qarnain, suggesting the author of the Quran did not have knowledge of a spherical earth.

Al-Qurtubi's Commentary

Al-Qurtubi's explanation further supports the flat-earth view:

"But it is meant that he reached the end of populated land east and west, so he found it—according to his vision—setting in a spring of murky water like we watch it in smooth land as if it enters inside the land."

This implies that the sun's movement was perceived as entering the land, a perspective that only makes sense on a flat earth. Additionally, the claim that the sun "rises first" on certain people reflects a flat-earth belief, as this is impossible on a spherical earth where the sun's light continuously moves around the rotating planet.

Conclusion

The story of Zul-Qarnain's travels in Surah 18:86 reveals two significant errors:

1. **The concept of an absolute east and west**: This reflects a flat-earth understanding and is incompatible with modern knowledge of a spherical earth.
2. **Contradictory points for extreme east and west**: Even if the Quranic descriptions are taken as relative rather than absolute, the two points would need to coincide on a globe, which the Quran does not acknowledge.

The traditional commentaries, such as those of al-Qurtubi, also reinforce these inaccuracies, demonstrating that early Islamic scholars largely operated under the assumption of a flat earth. This conclusion underscores the Quranic cosmology's incompatibility with modern scientific knowledge.

End of Populated Land: A Flat Earth Assumption?

The claim that Zul-Qarnain reached the "end of populated land" in the eastern and western directions raises significant questions. Early Muslim scholars, aware of seafaring and ships (as the Quran mentions them in numerous verses such as 2:164, 10:22, 14:32, and others), must have known that the seashore does not mark the actual end of populated land. By the time of these commentators, Muslims had sailed from Africa to Spain, and even earlier, some Muslims had fled from Mecca to Ethiopia by crossing the Red Sea (source). This awareness undermines the notion that populated land ends at the shoreline.

If one assumes an "end of populated land" in the east and west, it logically presupposes a flat earth. A spherical earth, by contrast, has no ultimate east or west; one can continue traveling indefinitely in either direction, eventually returning to the starting point.

Ibn Kathir's Commentary and Flat Earth Implications

Ibn Kathir's statement on the throne of Allah further reinforces the flat-earth assumption:

"... the Throne is the **roof** of creation and it is **not a sphere** as many astronomers claim. Rather, it is a **dome supported by legs or pillars**, carried by the angels, and it is **above the universe**, above the heads of people."

This perspective assumes that people exist only on one side of the earth, which must therefore be flat. Ibn Kathir explicitly denies the spherical nature of the throne because he feels constrained by the Quran and hadith, despite his attempts to reconcile Islamic teachings with scientific understanding where possible.

He also describes the sun as needing to ask permission to rise again after prostrating beneath the throne of Allah during the night. This notion requires a flat and stationary earth where the sun physically disappears (e.g., by dropping below the edge) rather than continuing its orbit around the globe. Al-Tabari elaborates on this process, suggesting a highly complex cosmology that defies modern scientific understanding.

The Influence of Pre-Islamic Astronomy

Interestingly, more than 800 years before Islam, the Greek astronomer Aristarchus of Samos (310–230 BCE) used basic trigonometry to calculate that:

1. The moon is about **60 times the radius of the earth** away, approximately 380,000 kilometers.
2. The sun is about **20 times larger in diameter than the moon** and significantly farther from the earth.
3. The earth orbits the sun, not the other way around.

These findings were based purely on observation and elementary mathematics, without any claim of divine revelation (source: istp.gsfc.nasa.gov). However, this advanced understanding of astronomy had not reached the Arabs of Muhammad's time. Despite adopting the idea that the sun is larger than the earth (as seen in interpretations by al-Jalalayn and al-Qurtubi), classical Muslim commentators maintained that the earth is flat and that the sun orbits it, constrained by Quranic descriptions and Islamic traditions.

Conclusion: Persistent Errors in Islamic Cosmology

The insistence on a flat earth and a geocentric model in classical Islamic interpretations highlights the limitations imposed by the Quran and hadith on scientific progress within early Islamic thought. While some commentators sought to reconcile Islamic teachings with emerging scientific knowledge, they ultimately deferred to Quranic descriptions that were scientifically inaccurate.

This contradiction between Quranic cosmology and scientific reality underscores the challenges faced by early Muslim scholars. Despite the advancements of pre-Islamic astronomy, Islamic traditions and interpretations clung to outdated cosmological views, unable to reconcile them fully with observable facts.

Acknowledgment

We extend gratitude to **Sam Shamoun** and **Jochen Katz** of *Answering Islam* for their exceptional analysis and insights into these issues.

CHAPTER 11

Many Sunrises .... Yet Still Awaiting Enlightenment

Harun Yahya's "scientific miracles of the Qur'an" section on his website (*miraclesofthequran.com*) has expanded to include 105 alleged miracles. The method of identifying a so-called scientific miracle typically involves three key elements:

1. **An interpretation of a Qur'anic verse**
2. **An explanation of a scientific fact**
3. **Establishing a connection between the two**

For a claim to qualify as a true scientific miracle, all three components must be accurate. A misinterpretation of the Qur'an or a distortion of scientific facts invalidates the claim. In my assessment, most of Yahya's claims fail because he often twists the meanings of Qur'anic verses to fabricate a miraculous association.

However, some of Yahya's claims demonstrate blatant ignorance of even basic scientific principles. One such example is his article on the "miracle" of the sun rising and setting from different points. Yahya writes:

Different Points of the Sun's Rising and Setting

"No! I swear by the Lord of the Easts and Wests that We have the power." (Qur'an, 70:40)
"Lord of the heavens and the earth and everything between them; Lord of the Easts." (Qur'an, 37:5)
"The Lord of the two Easts and the Lord of the two Wests." (Qur'an, 55:17)

"As can be discerned, the words *east* and *west* are used in the plural sense in the above verses. For instance, the word *mashariq* (used in the first verse for 'east') and the word *magharib* (used for 'west') are in the plural form, indicating that there are two of each. The words *mashriqayn* and *maghribayn* in the last verse refer to 'two easts' and 'two wests.' *Mashariq* and *magharib* also mean the places where the sun rises and sets. These verses therefore refer to different sites of the dawning and closing of the day. It is also noteworthy that the first verse takes an oath by the Lord of 'the easts and wests.'"

"The axis around which the earth revolves is tilted at an angle of 23° 27'. Due to this tilt and the earth's spherical shape, sunlight does not strike the earth at the same angle throughout the year. This tilt causes variations in the sun's rising and setting points. An observer far from the equator will notice the sun rising and setting at different points on the horizon throughout the year. The farther away one is from the equator, the greater the variation in the sun's apparent movement." (*miraclesofthequran.com*)

Errors in Yahya's Interpretation

Yahya's explanation contains significant inaccuracies and misrepresentations, betraying a lack of understanding of both linguistics and basic astronomy:

1. **Misinterpreting the plural forms** The plural forms *mashariq* (easts) and *magharib* (wests) do not imply "two of each," as Yahya claims. In Arabic grammar, the plural denotes *three or more*. For "two of something," Arabic employs the **dual form**, as seen in *mashriqayn* and *maghribayn* in Surah 55:17. By conflating the plural with the dual, Yahya fundamentally misunderstands the grammar.
2. **Misrepresenting the sun's rising and setting points** Yahya asserts that the sun's rising and setting points differ more significantly the farther one is from the equator. This is incorrect. Regardless of latitude, the number of distinct rising and setting points is the same, though they may appear closer together near the equator and more spread out at higher latitudes. Yahya also neglects to mention that these variations are caused by the earth's axial tilt, a phenomenon well-known in pre-Islamic times.

A Side Remark: An Oath or an Enigma?

In Surah 70:40, the Qur'an states:

"No! I swear by the Lord of the Easts and Wests that We have the power."

Yahya highlights this verse but fails to explain its significance. The verse introduces an intriguing question: **Who is speaking, and who are "We"?**

- The verse involves at least three entities: "I" (the speaker), "the Lord of the Easts and Wests," and "We."
- Is the speaker Allah, or is Allah the "Lord" mentioned separately?
- The ambiguity raises questions about clarity, undermining any claim of miraculous eloquence.

Conclusion

Harun Yahya's claim of a "scientific miracle" regarding the sun's rising and setting points collapses under scrutiny. His errors in interpreting Arabic grammar, his lack of understanding of basic astronomical principles, and his failure to coherently connect the Qur'anic verses to science demonstrate that his claims are neither scientific nor miraculous. Instead, they reflect a pattern of misinterpretation and pseudoscientific explanations that do more to confuse than to enlighten.

Exploring the Meaning of "Easts" and "Wests" in the Qur'an

Let's revisit the question of what the Qur'an might mean by the use of "Easts" and "Wests" in the dual or plural form. Ibn Abbas, a cousin of Muhammad and a renowned commentator on the Qur'an, offers the following explanation for Surah 55:17:

"Lord of the two Easts" refers to the East of winter and the East of summer, and **"Lord of the two Wests"** to the West of winter and the West of summer. There are two Easts and two Wests. The East of winter and the East of summer have 180 phases, just as the two Wests and the moon have 180 phases. It is also said that the Easts of summer and winter have 177 phases, and the Wests of summer and winter, as well as the moon, have 177 phases. The sun rises throughout the year on two days in the same phase and sets on two days in the same phase. *(Tanwîr al-Miqbâs min Tafsîr Ibn 'Abbâs; source: altafsir.com)*

Ibn Abbas explains the Qur'anic expression by connecting it to a phenomenon already familiar to people in his time: the sun rising and setting at different points throughout the year. His interpretation does not suggest that the Qur'an reveals a new, miraculous insight. Instead, it reflects an attempt to make sense of the verse using common knowledge.

Al-Tabari's Perspective

In his *Tafsir*, Al-Tabari (839-923 AD) adds further detail:

For the sun and the moon, Allah created easts and wests (points of rising and setting) on the two sides of the earth and the two rims of heaven, with 180 springs in the west of black clay—this is what is meant by God's words: "He found it setting in a muddy spring," where "muddy" (*hami'ah*) refers to black clay. Similarly, there are 180 springs in the east, also of black clay, bubbling and boiling like a pot. Each day and night, the sun has a new place where it rises and a new place where it sets. The interval between these points is longest during summer days and shortest in winter. This is what is meant by God's words: **"The Lord of the two Easts and the Lord of the two Wests"**—the furthest rising and setting points of the sun. He omitted the intermediate positions and later referred to them collectively as **"the Easts and the Wests."** (*The History of Al-Tabari: General Introduction and From the Creation to the Flood, translated by Franz Rosenthal, SUNY Press, Albany, 1989, Vol. 1, pp. 234-235)*

Ibn Kathir, Al-Jalalayn, and other classical commentators provide similar explanations. These interpretations indicate that the Qur'anic references to "Easts" and "Wests" simply reflect the observable phenomenon of the sun's varying positions throughout the year. There is nothing novel or scientifically groundbreaking in this explanation; such observations were common knowledge long before Muhammad's time.

A Question Raised Through Time

The expression "Easts and Wests" has prompted curiosity and discussion among Muslims and non-Muslims alike. From the earliest days of Islam, commentators have sought to explain this phrase in ways that align with observable reality. The explanation linking it to the sun's varying positions over the year has long been the dominant interpretation.

Harun Yahya's Claim

While traditional commentators accepted the natural explanation for these verses, Harun Yahya takes a different approach. Dissatisfied with a straightforward interpretation, Yahya insists on finding a miracle in every Qur'anic statement. In his effort to extract miraculous insight, Yahya writes:

Someone at the equator, however, will always observe that the Sun rises exactly in the east and sets exactly in the west, since the Sun's rays always fall perpendicularly there. Bearing in mind that the Arabian Peninsula is not that far from the equator, it would appear impossible for such an observation to be made there. That is because someone in that region would see that the Sun always rises at the same point and always sets at the same point.

Scientific Misstep

This claim is outright false and demonstrates Yahya's lack of understanding of basic scientific principles. The idea that someone near the equator would observe the sun rising and setting at the same points throughout the year is incorrect. Even at the equator, the sun's rising and setting points shift with the seasons due to the tilt of the earth's axis. Yahya's statement is either a product of ignorance or a deliberate attempt to mislead his audience by fabricating a "miracle" for the Qur'an.

A Misguided Search for Miracles

Yahya's eagerness to turn every Qur'anic expression into a scientific miracle undermines both the credibility of his claims and the Qur'anic text itself. While traditional commentators offered a reasonable explanation based on common knowledge of their time, Yahya's attempt to fabricate a scientific miracle reveals the lengths to which he will go to appeal to an audience seeking validation of their faith.

This misplaced enthusiasm highlights the danger of distorting scientific facts to fit a narrative, leaving readers with confusion rather than enlightenment.

Harun Yahya should easily recognize that there is a significant difference—more than 45 degrees—between the directions of the winter and summer sunrises. This discrepancy is readily observable and has been common knowledge since ancient times, as reflected in Ibn Abbas's commentary cited earlier.

However, it is always wise to verify claims made by any source, including Muslim missionary websites. Readers are encouraged to cross-check such assertions using reliable, independent tools. For example, solar calculators provided on scientific websites can confirm the accuracy of sunrise and sunset data.

Verifying Sunrise and Sunset Directions

Mecca is located at **Latitude 21.43°N, Longitude 39.82°E**, and is in the GMT +3 time zone (*source: greenwichmeantime.com*). Using a solar calculator, such as the one available at SpectralCalc, we can determine the azimuth of sunrise and sunset in Mecca for specific dates. The term "azimuth," as explained on the same website, refers to:

The angle measured clockwise (eastward) from true north to the point on the horizon directly below (or above) the object.

Here are the results for Mecca's location:

Date	21 June 2009 (Summer Solstice)	21 December 2009 (Winter Solstice)
Sunrise Azimuth	64.338°	114.938°
Sunset Azimuth	295.661°	245.060°

This data shows a difference of more than **50 degrees** between the summer and winter sunrise and sunset directions in Mecca. Harun Yahya's claim that such differences do not exist is demonstrably false.

Assessing Yahya's Claims About the Equator

Yahya's error extends beyond Mecca. Let's calculate sunrise and sunset azimuths at the equator (**Latitude 0°N, Longitude 39.82°E, GMT +3**):

Date	21 June 2009 (Summer Solstice)	21 December 2009 (Winter Solstice)
Sunrise Azimuth	66.558°	113.440°
Sunset Azimuth	293.441°	246.559°

The angles at the equator differ only slightly from those in Mecca, yet the difference between summer and winter sunrise and sunset directions remains greater than **45 degrees**.

Examining Yahya's Claim

Harun Yahya wrote:

Someone at the equator, however, will always observe that the Sun rises exactly in the east and sets exactly in the west, since the Sun's rays always fall perpendicularly there. Bearing in mind that the Arabian Peninsula is not that far from the equator, it would appear impossible for such an observation to be made there. That is because someone in that region would see that the Sun always rises at the same point and always sets at the same point.

This statement is entirely incorrect. Every sentence in this paragraph contradicts basic scientific facts.

Supporting Evidence

For clarity, consider this excerpt from **Wikipedia**:

On the equator the Sun is not overhead every day, as some people think. In fact, that happens only on two days of the year, the equinoxes. The solstices are the dates that the Sun stays farthest away from the zenith, only reaching an altitude of 66.56° either to the north or the south. The only thing special about the equator is that all days of the year, solstices included, have roughly the same length of about 12 hours, so that it makes no sense to talk about summer and winter. Instead, tropical areas often have wet and dry seasons. (Source: Solstice - Wikipedia; accessed 18 July 2009)

Final Thoughts

Is Harun Yahya genuinely ignorant of basic scientific principles, or does he intentionally mislead his audience to fabricate so-called "miracles of the Qur'an"? Either way, such flawed arguments damage his credibility and render his claims unworthy of serious consideration.

Footnote

1. Unless Harun Yahya wishes to argue that Muhammad neglected the dawn (*fajr*) prayer—a key Islamic obligation—Muhammad himself must have observed the shifting directions of the sunrise throughout the year. See this information on Islamic prayer.

C H A P T E R 1 2

The Scientific Miracle of the Moon's Date-Branch-Like Orbit

First, we would like to thank Al Hudhud for contributing to this discussion.

Recently, Osama Abdallah has promoted an argument online claiming the discovery of a "new scientific miracle" in the Qur'an. This claim, presented on his page *Moon's S-shaped orbit around Earth is shaped like a branch of a date tree, mentioned in the Noble Quran and confirmed by Science!* (answering-christianity.com), is rooted in an interpretation that appears to have originated from Harun Yahya.

Harun Yahya and others argue that the Qur'an contains scientific facts unknown during Muhammad's time, thereby proving it to be divinely inspired. Specifically, this argument claims that **Surah 36:39** predicts modern scientific knowledge about the moon's orbit, something allegedly beyond the understanding of people in Muhammad's era.

The Claim

Surah 36:39, in a word-for-word translation, reads:

"And the moon We predestined/evaluated it (in) sequences/descents until it returned as/like the palm tree's branch/date bunch, the old."

According to Osama Abdallah, this verse describes the moon's orbit around Earth as an **S-shaped path**, resembling the shape of an old palm tree branch. He asserts that this observation, confirmed by modern science, was miraculously predicted in the Qur'an.

Agreement and Clarifications

Before examining the claim in detail, let us acknowledge some points of agreement:

1. **The Moon's Complex Orbit** Modern science indeed confirms that the moon's elliptical orbit around Earth exhibits lateral variations due to several factors:
   - The moon's orbital plane is tilted by about **5.1°** relative to Earth's equatorial plane.
   - The intersection line of these planes undergoes precession (rotation) over **18.6 years** due to nutation.
   - Earth's equatorial plane itself is tilted by **23.4°** relative to the ecliptic plane, with a slow precession cycle of **25,800 years**.

These combined effects create a three-dimensional spiral path for the moon, resembling a twisted "S" shape when mapped over time. Thus, the moon's path deviates from a simple circular or elliptical trajectory, forming a complex, oscillating pattern in space.

2. **Common Observations in History** This knowledge is not exclusive to modern times. Ancient civilizations had already observed and recorded irregularities in the moon's movement.

Two Critical Questions

To evaluate this claim thoroughly, we must address the following:

1. **Was this "S-shaped" motion of the moon unknown to humanity before Muhammad's time (6th–7th century CE)?**
2. **Does Surah 36:39 explicitly describe the moon's orbit in scientific terms, including its S-shaped path?**

Question 1: Historical Knowledge of the Moon's Orbit

Evidence shows that the moon's complex motion was well-known long before Muhammad's time:

- **Babylonian Astronomy (6th Century BCE):** Ancient Babylonian texts reveal that astronomers observed variations in the moon's speed and lateral position. Documents such as *MUL.APIN* (dated as early as 1000 BCE) detail lunar and solar cycles, eclipses, and celestial movements.
- **Greek Astronomy:**
    - **Hipparchus (190–120 BCE):** Developed a mathematical theory of the moon's orbit, incorporating precession and non-circular motion.
    - **Ptolemy (83–161 CE):** Refined Hipparchus's work in his *Almagest*, introducing epicyclic models to explain the moon's irregular path.

Islamic astronomers later translated and preserved these works, using them as a foundation for further studies. Thus, the moon's non-circular motion was well-documented centuries before the Qur'an.

Question 2: Interpretation of Surah 36:39

Does Surah 36:39 explicitly describe the moon's S-shaped orbit? A closer analysis reveals that this claim is speculative at best:

- **Literal Meaning:** The verse metaphorically compares the moon's phases or appearance to an "old date palm branch," likely referring to its crescent shape during waning phases.
- **Stretching the Interpretation:** Abdallah attempts to reinterpret "date branch" as an analogy for the moon's orbital path, but this is not a natural reading of the text. The verse neither mentions orbits nor provides any indication of the moon's three-dimensional trajectory.
- **Historical Context:** Early Qur'anic commentators like Ibn Abbas interpreted the verse in terms of the moon's observable changes in shape (phases), not its orbital path. These interpretations align with common knowledge of the time.

Analysis of Abdallah's Claims

Abdallah asserts that the moon's S-shaped orbit was an unknown fact revealed in the Qur'an. However:

- **Ancient Knowledge:** Historical evidence shows that the moon's irregular motion was already well-understood by Babylonian and Greek astronomers centuries before Muhammad.
- **Misinterpretation of the Verse:** The verse likely refers to the moon's phases, not its orbital path. Abdallah's interpretation imposes modern scientific concepts onto a metaphorical description.

Conclusion

The claim that Surah 36:39 predicts the moon's S-shaped orbit is unfounded. Historical records demonstrate that such knowledge predates the Qur'an, while the verse itself is more reasonably interpreted as a reference to the moon's phases.

Harun Yahya and Osama Abdallah's insistence on finding "scientific miracles" in the Qur'an often leads to exaggerated claims and misinterpretations of both the Qur'an and science. These approaches do more harm than good to their credibility.

The precession of the moon in its movement around the Earth was well-known for centuries, if not millennia, before Muhammad's time. All Muhammad would have needed to do was listen to a conversation among astronomers of his era to learn about it.

Furthermore, the video available on Osama Abdallah's website, titled *"The Universe is Full of Paths and Orbits,"* which refers to Surah 51:7 (*"By the sky full of paths and orbits"*), also fails to provide convincing evidence of the Qur'an's divine origin. The notion that celestial bodies follow paths and orbits was already well-established long before Muhammad's time, and such observations would have been apparent even within a geocentric model of the universe.

Analysis of Surah 36:39

Surah 36:37–40 emphasizes the alternation between daylight and the darkness of night as signs for human reflection. Verse 39, in particular, seems to focus on the phases of the moon, which wax from a crescent to a full moon and then wane back to a thin crescent.

Imagine standing in the Arabian desert during a night near the new moon, where the moon appears as a thin crescent. A person near an old, dry palm tree could easily position themselves so that a curved date palm branch visually aligns with the crescent moon, both exhibiting a similar curved shape. This provides a plausible and natural explanation for the comparison in the verse, likening the weak crescent moon to the curved, thin shape of a dry palm branch.

There is, however, no clear indication in the verse that it refers to the spatial orbit of the moon. On the contrary, if these verses were meant to describe the moon's orbital path, one could ask why the Qur'an does not mention the moon's proximity to the sun during a solar eclipse—a phenomenon that could have provided a more striking example of the moon's path.

Thus, the interpretation that Surah 36:39 refers to the scientific "miracle" of the moon's S-shaped orbital path requires inserting modern concepts into the text (*eisegesis*) rather than deriving them from the text's natural meaning (*exegesis*).

Vagueness of the Date Palm Comparison

The claim that the shape of an old date palm branch symbolizes the S-shaped orbital path of the moon is, at best, speculative. This analogy is too vague to be considered evidence of advanced scientific knowledge unknown during Muhammad's time. The text offers no explicit reference to orbital mechanics or spatial movement, making such interpretations highly tenuous.

Conclusion

1. The precession movement of the moon (which could be interpreted as somewhat S-shaped) was already known centuries before Muhammad.
2. The wording of Surah 36:39 is far too vague to support claims of a scientific "miracle." The idea of the date palm-shaped

orbital path of the moon must be imposed on the text, rather than arising naturally from it.

Ultimately, the argument for this "scientific miracle" fails to hold up under scrutiny, relying on ambiguous interpretations and disregarding historical and scientific knowledge available long before the Qur'an was revealed.

CHAPTER 13

The Thunder and the Moon

Examples of "Islamic Science" Fiction

Sam Shamoun from *Answering Islam* offers the following response to the claim that the Qur'an suggests thunder is an angel:

Is Thunder an Angel?

The Qur'an states that thunder glorifies Allah:

And Ar-Ra'd (thunder) glorifies and praises Him, and so do the angels because of His Awe. He sends the thunderbolts, and therewith He strikes whom He wills, yet they (disbelievers) dispute about Allah. And

He is Mighty in strength and Severe in punishment. (S. 13:13 Hilali Khan)

At first glance, one might interpret this verse poetically, ascribing a form of personification to thunder to emphasize how it fulfills its divinely intended purpose. However, upon examining Islamic commentaries, it becomes evident that the Qur'anic author and early Muslim scholars regarded thunder as more than just a natural phenomenon—they believed it to be an angel.

Tafsir Ibn Abbas

According to *Tanwîr al-Miqbâs min Tafsîr Ibn 'Abbâs,* this verse explicitly identifies thunder as an angel:

The thunder hymneth His praise by His command; it is an angel. It is also said: it is the voice of the sky... He launches the thunderbolts (fire) and smites with them whom He will, referring here to Zayd Ibn Qays, whom Allah destroyed by fire, along with his friend 'Amir Ibn al-Tufayl, who was killed as a result of being stabbed in his waist...

Tafsir al-Jalalayn

The two Jalals elaborate further:

The thunder—this is an angel in charge of the clouds, driving them— constantly proclaims His praise. That is, it says, 'Glory be to God through His praise.' And so too the angels proclaim His praise in awe of Him. He unleashes the thunderbolts—fire from the clouds—and smites with them whom He wills, such that it burns [the person]. This was revealed regarding a man who mocked the Prophet by asking, 'What is Allah? Is He made of gold or silver?' A thunderbolt struck and killed him...

Additional Commentary

The Hilali-Khan translation cites *Tafsir al-Qurtubi:*

(V.13:13) Ar-Ra'd: It is said that he is the angel in charge of clouds. He drives them as ordered by Allah and glorifies His praises.

Further, Christian apologist 'Abdallah 'Abd al-Fadi quotes *al-Baidawi* and *al-Tirmidhi:*

- *Al-Baidawi:*

  The Prophet was asked about thunder. He answered, "It is an angel entrusted with the clouds. He drives the clouds with shreds of fire."

- *Al-Tirmidhi:*

  The Jews came to Muhammad and asked, "Tell us about the thunder. What is it?" He replied, "It is an angel entrusted with the clouds. The sound you hear is his rebuke to the clouds, commanding them to stop where they have been ordered."

Scientific Reality

The problem with these claims lies in the scientific explanation of thunder and lightning. Thunder is not an independent entity or an angel; it is a natural phenomenon caused by lightning. Specifically:

- Lightning heats the air around it to extreme temperatures (up to 30,000°C or 54,000°F).
- This rapid heating causes the air to expand explosively, creating a shockwave.

- As the air cools and contracts, it generates sound waves—what we call thunder.

Thus, thunder is simply a byproduct of lightning, not an independent force or being.

Conclusion

The interpretation that thunder is an angel reflects the pre-scientific worldview of the Qur'an's time. While such explanations may have been accepted historically, modern science has conclusively demonstrated that thunder and lightning are purely physical phenomena. As such, claims that the Qur'an contains miraculous scientific knowledge about thunder fall apart under scrutiny, revealing instead the limitations of the knowledge available to the author and commentators of the Qur'an.

Thunder and Moon: Scientific Misunderstandings in the Quran

Thunder and Clouds

No physicist or meteorologist would agree with the claim that thunder drives clouds. Scientifically, it is the wind—caused by differences in temperature and atmospheric pressure—that moves clouds (source: Wikipedia). Thunder, being the sound produced by the rapid expansion and contraction of air heated by lightning, has no influence on cloud movement and cannot cause clouds to stop or change direction.

The Moon's Movement

The Quran describes the moon as traveling on a predetermined course throughout space:

And the moon, We have measured for it mansions (to traverse) till it returns like the old dried curved date stalk. It is not permitted to the Sun to catch up the Moon, nor can the Night outstrip the Day: Each (just) swims along in (its own) orbit (according to Law). (S. 36:39-40 Hilali-Khan)

Commentaries on the Moon's Course

According to the Tafsir al-Jalalayn:

And the moon - We have determined it [to run] in phases, twenty-eight phases over twenty-eight nights each month. For two nights (if the month has 30 days) or one night (if the month has 29 days), the moon is concealed. During its final phase, it appears to the human eye like an aged palm-bough—delicate, arched, and yellowish.

Abd al-Fadi quotes *al-Baidawi* to explain the Quranic description further:

"The moon—we determined" means its course is determined by 27 stations, including Saratan ('Cancer'), Thurayya ('the Pleiades'), and others. Each night the moon is said to rest at one station without exceeding or delaying its arrival. When it reaches its final station before the conjunction, it tapers and appears like an old palm frond. "It behoves not the sun" indicates that the sun cannot overtake the moon in speed, nor does the night precede the day. Each celestial body swims effortlessly in its orbit.

Scientific Reality

Contrary to the Quran's implication, modern science reveals the following:

1. The moon does not traverse space in the manner described but revolves around the Earth in a continuous elliptical orbit, completing one revolution in approximately 29.5 days.

2. The idea that the moon "rests" at specific stations is incorrect. The moon's motion is continuous and governed by gravitational forces.

Conclusion

The Quran's descriptions of the moon's movement and thunder's influence on clouds reflect a pre-scientific worldview rather than divine insight. The moon does not "rest" at stations, nor does it traverse "throughout space" as the Quran suggests. Instead, it follows a well-understood orbital path around Earth.

These inaccuracies, along with the scientifically erroneous claim about thunder moving clouds, serve as additional evidence that the Quran is not the Word of God but rather a reflection of the cosmological and natural understanding of the time.

CHAPTER 14
Astronomy and the Quran

Claims of Scientific Accuracy

Some Muslims assert that the Qur'an contains scientific truths regarding the orbits of the sun, moon, and sometimes planets. While this claim is intriguing, a closer examination reveals that unless one interprets these verses as describing the phenomena from the perspective of human appearance, they could disprove, rather than confirm, the scientific accuracy of the Qur'an.

Key Verses for Analysis

Sura 36:37-40 states:

"And a sign for them is the night: We withdraw therefrom the day, and behold they are plunged in darkness; and the sun runs its course for a period determined for it; that is the decree of (Him), the Exalted in Might, the All-Knowing. And the moon—we have measured for it mansions (to traverse) till it returns like the old (and withered) lower

part of a date stalk. It is not permitted to the sun to catch up the moon, nor can the night outstrip the day: Each (just) swims along in (its own) orbit (according to law)." (Yusuf Ali's original translation; parenthetical additions are from the translator.)

Some Muslims highlight the phrases *"the sun runs its course"* and *"swims along in its own orbit"* as evidence of scientific accuracy. However, Yusuf Ali's own footnote clarifies that *"orbit"* can mean *"circuit"* or *"course,"* and his revised translation replaces *"period determined"* with *"resting place."*

Translation and Interpretation Issues

Certain interpretations take liberties with the text. For example, the Sufi site **modern_science_and_islam** adds phrases like *(all of them are planets)* and *(or on their axis)* to imply modern scientific concepts. These additions, however, are not present in the Arabic text and should be dismissed as overly loose interpretations.

Three Interpretative Possibilities

1. **Orbits of the Sun and Moon**: The Qur'an teaches that the sun and moon follow continuous paths around the Earth with specific, ordained periods.
2. **Swim to a Resting Place**: The sun moves across the sky during the day and returns to a "resting place" at night, resuming its course the next dawn.
3. **Language of Appearance**: The verses describe the apparent movement of celestial bodies as observed from Earth, rather than their actual behavior.

Examining the Arabic

- **Course/Orbit**: Yusuf Ali's footnote explains that the Arabic *mustaqarr* can mean *"a limit of time," "a resting place,"* or *"a* *dwelling place."* Some commentators suggest it describes the sun's perceived journey across the sky, resting at night.

- **Move/Swim/Rotate**: The Arabic *yasbahuna* translates to "swimming" or "hastening along."
- **Celestial Spheres**: Ibn Taymiyyah (died 1328 A.D.) mentioned celestial bodies as "round" and swimming in "falak," which he interpreted as circular or spherical motion.

Scientific Misalignment

- The Arabic term *mahrek,* not *falak,* describes an orbit in modern understanding.
- The word *falak* predates the Qur'an, borrowed from other Semitic languages to describe celestial motions within the "sky dome."

Ancient people, including Arabs and those influenced by Aristotelian and Ptolemaic models, believed the Earth was at the center of seven concentric spheres. The Qur'an's reference to "seven heavens" aligns more closely with these pre-scientific models than with modern astronomy.

Conclusions

1. The Qur'an's description of celestial movements reflects ideas already known before Muhammad's time.
2. The text is vague and open to interpretation, with no clear evidence of uniquely advanced scientific insights.
3. If the early Muslims understood these verses as describing celestial orbits, their interpretations align with pre-scientific models rather than modern astronomy.

To evaluate claims of scientific miracles in the Qur'an, it is essential to consider the historical and cultural context of its composition. At best, these verses describe celestial phenomena as they appeared to observers in Muhammad's era, without presenting groundbreaking scientific knowledge.

What Muhammad and Early Muslims Said About the Sun

To understand the Qur'an's intended meaning, early Muslims would have relied directly on Muhammad's explanations. Here's what Muhammad and prominent Islamic scholars, including al-Tabari, said about the sun:

Muhammad's Explanation of the Sun's Setting

From *Sahih al-Bukhari* and *al-Tabari*:

1. **Narrated Abu Dhar:**

   "The Prophet asked me at sunset, 'Do you know where the sun goes (at the time of sunset)?' I replied, 'Allah and His Apostle know best.' He said, 'It goes (i.e., travels) till it prostrates itself underneath the Throne and seeks permission to rise again. A time will come when it will be about to prostrate itself, but its prostration will not be accepted...'" (*Sahih al-Bukhari*, vol. 4, book 54, no. 441).

2. **Another Translation of the Same Hadith:**

   "Abu Dharr narrated: One day Prophet Muhammad (peace be upon him) asked me, 'Abu Dharr, do you know where the sun goes after setting?' I replied, 'I do not know. Only Allah and His Apostle can say.' Then the Prophet said, 'After setting, the sun prostrates under Allah's Throne and waits for His command to rise again in the East. A day will come when it will not be permitted to rise again, and the Day of Judgment will begin.'"

Al-Tabari's Interpretation

Al-Tabari elaborates further:

- **On the Sun's Journey and Prostration:**

"I asked the Messenger of God [Muhammad], 'Where does the sun set?' He replied: 'It sets in the heaven and is then raised from heaven to heaven until it reaches the highest, seventh heaven. Eventually, it prostrates itself under the Throne, along with the angels in charge of it. The sun then asks, "My Lord, from where do You command me to rise—where I set, or where I rose before?" This is what is meant by God's words: "And the sun runs to a resting place for it. That is the decree of the Mighty, the Knowing."'"

- **On the Sun's Garments of Light:**

"Gabriel brings the sun a garment of luminosity from the light of the Throne, according to the measure of the hours of the day. In summer, it is longer; in winter, it is shorter; and in autumn and spring, it is of intermediate length. The sun dons this garment, as one of you dons clothing, and then roams in the air of heaven until it rises again."

Additional Teachings

1. **The Sun and Moon as Signs of Allah:**

"The sun and moon are signs of Allah." (*Sunan Abu Dawood*, vol. 1, book 2, no. 1173; *Sunan an-Nasa'i*, vol. 2, multiple references).

2. **Zul-Qarnain and the Sun's Setting:**

"Zul-Qarnain witnessed the sun setting in its resting place, a pool of black and fetid slime." (*Al-Tabari*, vol. 5, p. 173-174; related to Qur'an 18:86).

3. **Eclipses and the Sun Falling into the Deep Ocean:**

"When God wishes to test the sun and the moon, the sun tumbles from its chariot and falls into the deep of the ocean, which is the sphere. This total eclipse darkens the day, and stars become visible. When the sun rises again, it does so from one of its springs, accompanied by 360 angels." (*Al-Tabari*, vol. 1, p. 236).

Key Observations

- **Prostration of the Sun:** Muhammad taught that the sun prostrates under Allah's Throne at night, awaiting permission to rise again.
- **Resting Place:** The sun's "resting place" is described as beneath Allah's Throne, aligning with the Qur'anic verses interpreted literally.
- **Eclipse Interpretation:** Eclipses were described as the sun falling into the deep ocean and being removed from its chariot.

Conclusion

These interpretations reflect a pre-scientific cosmology, consistent with ancient beliefs that celestial bodies physically move in relation to the Earth and perform actions like prostration. While poetic or metaphorical readings might align with modern perspectives, the early explanations by Muhammad and Islamic scholars suggest a literal understanding that contradicts contemporary astronomical knowledge.

What Muhammad and Early Muslims Believed About the Heavens

Early Islamic Beliefs on the Sun, Moon, and Stars

1. **The Five "Retrograde Stars" (Planets):** Al-Tabari explains:

"The Prophet [Muhammad] replied, 'Ali, they are five stars: Jupiter (al-Birjis), Saturn (Zuhal), Mercury ('Utarid), Mars (Bahram), and Venus (al-Zuhrah). These five stars rise and run like the sun and the moon and race with them together. All the other stars are suspended from heaven as lamps are from

mosques.'"
(*Al-Tabari*, vol. 1, p. 235-236)

2. **An Ocean Above the Heavens:** Al-Tabari also described a celestial ocean:

"God created an ocean three fasrakhs (18 kilometers) removed from heaven. Its waves are contained, standing in the air by God's command, and not a single drop spills. All the oceans on earth are motionless, but that ocean flows at the speed of an arrow, stretched out evenly in the space between east and west. The sun, moon, and the five retrograde stars swim in its deep swell. This is what is meant by God's word: 'Each swims in a sphere.' 'The sphere' is the circulation of the chariot in the deep swell of that ocean." (*Al-Tabari*, vol. 1, p. 235)

Conclusion from Early Islamic Sources: Early Muslim interpretations present a cosmology where:

- The sun literally sets in a specific place (a muddy spring) and moves along a defined path.
- The sun and moon "swim" in a celestial ocean.
- The stars (except for the five planets) are suspended like lamps in the sky.

What the Qur'an Says About the Heavens and the Earth

Descriptions of the Earth

1. **The Earth as a Carpet:**
    o *Sura 20:53*:

        "He who has made for you the earth like a carpet spread out."

- *Sura 71:19*:

  "And Allah has made the earth for you as a carpet (spread out)." Yusuf Ali comments:

2. "The earth appears as a vast expanse, like a carpet, kept steady with the weight of the mountains."
3. **Manageable Earth:**
   - *Sura 67:15*:

     "It is He who has made the earth manageable..." Yusuf Ali notes that the Arabic term "zalul" can also mean "level," describing the earth as tractable and steady.

4. **Mountains as Pegs:**
   - *Sura 78:6-7*:

     "Have We [Allah] not made the earth as a wide expanse, and the mountains as pegs?"

Descriptions of the Sun and Moon

1. **Zul-Qarnain and the Sun's Setting:**
   - *Sura 18:85-86*:

     "He [Zul-Qarnain] followed a path, until, when he reached the setting of the sun, he found it set in a spring of murky water, and nearby he found a people." "Murky" has been translated as "muddy" or "black," and "spring" as "body of water" in some interpretations.

2. **The Sun's Rising Point:**
   - *Sura 18:89-90*:

     "Then he followed another path, until when he came to the rising of the sun, he found it rising on a people for whom We had provided no covering protection against it."

3. **The Sun and Moon's Path:**
   o *Sura 36:39-40*:

   "And the moon – We have measured for it mansions (to traverse) till it returns like the old dried curved date stalk. It is not permitted to the sun to catch up the moon, nor can the night outstrip the day: each swims along in its orbit."

Analysis of the Qur'anic Cosmology

1. **Flat Earth Imagery:** The Qur'an repeatedly describes the earth as "spread out like a carpet" and "manageable," with mountains acting as pegs. While some argue these descriptions are metaphorical, early interpretations suggest a literal understanding of a flat, stable earth.
2. **The Sun's Setting Place:** *Sura 18* describes the sun setting in a muddy spring and rising from a specific spot, which supports a flat-earth cosmology rather than modern astronomical understanding.
3. **Stars as Lamps:** The Qur'an describes stars as suspended like lamps, an idea consistent with pre-modern beliefs of a dome-like sky but inconsistent with contemporary astronomy.

Conclusion

The Qur'anic depiction of the earth, sun, moon, and stars aligns with ancient cosmological views rather than modern science. According to these interpretations:

- The earth is flat and pegged by mountains.
- The sun follows a defined path, setting in a muddy spring and rising from a fixed location.
- Stars are suspended as lamps, except for five retrograde stars (planets) that move independently.

Early Muslims, including Muhammad himself, taught these views as literal truths. These descriptions reflect the knowledge and beliefs of the time but contradict modern scientific understanding, challenging claims that the Qur'an contains advanced scientific insights.

The Purpose of Stars and Meteors in Islamic Tradition

Stars as Decorations and Missiles:

- The Qur'an states the purpose of stars in *Sura 67:5*:

  "The lowest heaven has lamps [stars], and 'We have made such (Lamps) (as) missiles to drive away the Evil ones, and have prepared for them the Penalty of the Blazing Fire.'"

- According to *Sahih Bukhari*:

  "The creation of these stars is for three purposes, i.e., as decoration of the sky, as missiles to hit the devils, and as signs to guide travelers. So, if anybody tries to find a different interpretation, he is mistaken and just wastes his efforts..." (*Bukhari*, vol. 4, book 54, ch. 3, before no. 421, p. 282).

- Shooting stars are described as being hurled at devils who attempt to eavesdrop on heavenly secrets: (*Sahih Muslim*, vol. 1, book 4, no. 902, footnote 674, p. 243).
- Shooting stars are also said to target bad angels before they spread what they have overheard, though some soothsayers might still receive messages before the angels are struck: (*Ibn-i-Majah*, vol. 1, book 1, no. 194, p. 110).

- Meteors are described as weapons used to attack *jinn* (genies): (*Sahih Muslim*, vol. 4, book 24, no. 5538, p. 1210).
- Stars are seen as guardians against Satan: (*al-Tabari*, vol. 1, p. 223).

The Splitting of the Moon

Accounts of the Miracle:

- Multiple narrations in *Sahih Bukhari* record the Prophet Muhammad performing the miracle of splitting the moon into two halves:

  "The Prophet showed them the splitting of the moon. Narrated 'Abdullah bin Masud: During the lifetime of the Prophet, the moon was split into two parts, and on that, the Prophet said, 'Bear witness (to this).'" (*Bukhari*, vol. 4, book 56, ch. 26, no. 830, p. 533).

- Another narration from *Anas*:

  "The Meccan people requested Allah's Apostle to show them a miracle, and so he showed them the splitting of the moon." (*Bukhari*, vol. 4, book 56, no. 831, p. 533).

- Further confirmations of this event are found in: *Bukhari* (vol. 6, book 60, no. 290, 345, 368-370, 387-391) and *Sahih Muslim* (vol. 4, book 37, no. 6721-6730, pp. 1467-1468).

Qur'anic Reference:

- *Sura 54:1*:

  "The Hour (of Judgment) is nigh, and the moon was cleft asunder."

This verse uses the past tense, indicating the splitting of the moon had already occurred.

Interpretations and Issues:

- **Three Interpretations by Yusuf 'Ali** (*Footnote 5128*):
    1. The moon was physically cleft asunder in the valley of Mecca, witnessed by Muhammad, his companions, and disbelievers.
    2. The past tense signifies a prophetic reference to a future event, possibly a sign of the approaching Day of Judgment.
    3. The phrase is metaphorical, symbolizing clarity akin to the brightness of the moon.
- The first explanation suggests the moon physically split, witnessed by those present. However, there are **no historical records from other civilizations**—such as Egypt, Syria, or Persia—documenting this phenomenon, despite the proximity of these regions to Arabia.
- Additionally, the Qur'an and hadiths do not explain how the moon was restored to its original form after being split.

Astronomical Observatories:

As a side note, the *Encyclopaedia Britannica* (*vol. 13, 1972, p. 458B*) features an image of the Chomsungdae astronomical observatory in Korea, built during the 7th-century Silla period. This shows that astronomical phenomena were being studied and documented worldwide during this era, yet no records of the moon splitting exist.

Conclusion

The Islamic traditions present stars and meteors as decorative elements, signs for travelers, and weapons against devils, bad angels, and *jinn*. The splitting of the moon is described as a miracle performed by Muhammad, but there is no independent corroboration from other civilizations or contemporary observers. These descriptions align with the cosmological beliefs of the time but lack consistency with modern scientific understanding.

Counter-Examples in the Qur'an: Claims of Astronomical Knowledge

Some Muslims claim that certain verses in the Qur'an demonstrate advanced astronomical understanding. Below are some commonly cited verses and responses to their claims:

---

1. Day and Night in Rapid Succession

Sura 7:54:

"...He draweth the night as a veil o'er the day, each seeking the other in rapid succession:..."

Response:
While it is true that day and night follow each other, this observation was obvious to ancient people. There is nothing here that suggests advanced astronomical knowledge.

---

2. Heavens Without Pillars

Sura 13:2a and Sura 31:10:

"...Allah raised the heavens without any pillars that you can see."

Response:
While not all ancient cultures believed the heavens were held up by pillars, this verse merely states that Allah did not use visible pillars. This is a poetic description, not a scientific insight.

3. Sun and Moon Run Their Courses

Sura 13:2b:

"...He has subjected the sun and the moon! Each one runs (its course) for a term appointed."

Response:
The regularity of the sun and moon's movements was well known to ancient peoples. There is no new scientific knowledge in this statement.

4. Heaven and Earth Were Once One

Sura 21:30:

"Do not the Unbelievers see that the heavens and the earth were jointed together (as one Unit of Creation), before we [Allah] clove them asunder?"

Muslim Claim: This verse anticipates the Big Bang theory.

Response:
Similar concepts existed in ancient mythologies, such as those of the Egyptians and Aryan Hindus, who believed the heavens and earth were initially together before being separated. The Qur'an's description aligns more closely with these ancient myths than with the Big Bang theory.

5. Celestial Bodies Swimming in Orbits

Sura 21:33:

"All (the celestial bodies) swim along, each in its rounded course."

Response:
The term "swim" is a metaphorical description. Classical commentators, such as al-Tabari, understood this to refer only to the sun, moon, and retrograde stars (planets). The inclusion of "(celestial bodies)" in some translations adds a modern interpretation not present in the original Arabic.

6. Rolling Up the Heavens

Sura 21:104:

"The day that We roll up the heavens like a scroll."

Response:
This phrase is similar to biblical imagery found in *Revelation 6:14* and *Isaiah 34:4*. There is no evidence that this anticipates any modern astronomical theory.

7. Withholding the Sky

Sura 22:65:

"...He withholds the sky from falling on the earth except by His leave..."

Response:
Yusuf Ali notes that the word *samaa* can mean sky, canopy, or cloud.

Many authorities translate it as "sky," consistent with a flat-earth cosmology. This verse does not suggest any advanced understanding of the atmosphere or gravity.

8. Sun, Moon, and Constellations

Sura 25:61-62:

"Blessed is He who made constellations in the skies, and placed therein a lamp and a moon giving light. And it is He who made the night and the day to follow each other."

Response:
Describing the sun as a lamp and the night and day following each other reflects common observations of the time, not advanced astronomy.

9. Moving Mountains

Sura 27:88:

"...these mountains which you see and think are firmly fixed, will pass away like clouds..."

Response:
This verse refers to the end times, as the preceding verse mentions the last trumpet. It is unrelated to the earth's rotation or tectonic plate movement.

10. Merging of Night and Day

Sura 31:29, Sura 35:13, Sura 36:37, Sura 39:5:

Allah merges night into day and day into night.

Sura 55:5:

The sun and moon run their appointed courses.

Response:
The merging of night and day reflects the observable transition of light and darkness. These verses say nothing about the earth's rotation or any other modern scientific understanding. Ancient peoples observed the same phenomena.

---

11. Creation as a Sign

Sura 29:44:

"The creation of the heavens and the earth is a sign for those who believe."

Response:
The creation of the heavens and earth has always been a source of awe and inspiration, as seen in *Psalm 19:1-6* and *Psalm 8:1-3, 5*. This verse does not suggest any scientific insight unique to the Qur'an.

Conclusion

While the Qur'an contains poetic and metaphorical language about the heavens, sun, moon, and stars, these verses reflect the observational knowledge of ancient peoples rather than advanced scientific understanding. Attempting to reinterpret these verses as precursors to modern astronomy often requires reading meanings into the text that were not present in its original context.

Reinterpretation of Astronomical Claims in the Qur'an

Sura 51:47-48

"We have built the firmament with might: and We indeed have vast power. And we have spread out the (spacious) earth: how excellently We do spread out!" (Yusuf Ali). Other translations use the phrase "like a carpet."

Response:
The phrase "spreading out the earth" has been interpreted by some as suggesting a flat earth, though it could also be understood as poetic language. Claiming that this refers to modern scientific theories, such as the Big Bang or the expansion of the universe, is a stretch. The phrase does not explicitly refer to cosmic expansion and is similar to biblical language, such as in *Isaiah 42:5*, which speaks of God stretching out the heavens. However, Christians do not typically use such vague references to claim anticipation of the Big Bang theory.

Sura 55:33

Mentions zones of the earth and heavens that men and Jinns cannot pass without divine authority.

Response:
This does not necessarily teach modern geography. Instead, it implies barriers, perhaps akin to mythical boundaries, that limit travel across zones of the earth or heaven. Both the Qur'an and Jewish tradition mention the concept of "seven heavens," but these references lack specificity in a scientific sense.

Sura 71:15-16

"See ye not how Allah has created the seven heavens one above another, And made the moon a light in the midst, and made the sun as a (Glorious) lamp?"

Claim: Some Muslims interpret the seven heavens as the seven layers of the earth's atmosphere (troposphere, stratosphere, etc.).

Response:
The notion of seven heavens predates Islam and aligns with Jewish traditions. Describing the moon as a "light" and the sun as a "lamp" does not suggest advanced scientific knowledge, though it is not incorrect if understood as poetic language. However, if the seven heavens refer to atmospheric layers, it would be inaccurate to claim the sun, moon, and stars exist within these layers.

Side Note: Apocryphal Jewish works, such as *2 Enoch*, *The Testament of the Twelve Patriarchs*, and *3 Baruch*, also reference seven heavens. If the Qur'an's mention of seven heavens were a scientific miracle, these earlier texts would be equally miraculous.

Sura 86:1-3

"By the heaven and by the visitant by night, and what will explain to you what the visitant by night is? It is the star of piercing brightness."

Claim: Some Muslims argue this verse implies that the sun is a star.

Response:
The sun is not mentioned here, and everything in parentheses in some translations (e.g., "Just as Allah Almighty is taking care of each star in

the galaxies...") is an addition by translators, not found in the original Arabic.

Accurate Translation (Yusuf Ali):

"By the Sky and the Night-Visitant (therein); And what will explain to thee what the Night-Visitant is? (It is) the Star of piercing brightness; - there is no soul but has a protector over it."

Footnote (Yusuf Ali): The "Star of piercing brightness" has been interpreted variously as the Morning Star, Saturn, Sirius, or the Pleiades. However, the verse likely refers to stars collectively or generically, emphasizing their brightness rather than making any specific astronomical claim.

Summary of Responses

1. **Sura 51:47-48**: While poetic, the claim of cosmic expansion is speculative and not explicit.
2. **Sura 55:33**: Mentions zones of the earth and heaven but does not teach modern geography or astronomy.
3. **Sura 71:15-16**: References seven heavens and celestial objects but aligns more with earlier traditions than modern science.
4. **Sura 86:1-3**: Does not specifically refer to the sun as a star, and interpretations about celestial details remain vague.

Overall, while the Qur'an contains poetic descriptions of the heavens and celestial bodies, the scientific interpretations often rely on modern readings into ancient texts rather than deriving scientific truths directly from the original language or intent.

Far-Fetched Interpretations of the Qur'an

The website debate.org.uk records some intriguing and highly speculative interpretations of the Qur'an. According to this source, certain individuals have claimed to find modern scientific advancements and technologies embedded within the Qur'anic verses. Here are some examples:

1. **Muhammad Hanafi al-Banna**: He allegedly discovered references to aeroplanes (Sura 17:1), artificial satellites (Sura 41:53), interplanetary travel (Sura 55:33), and even the hydrogen bomb (Sura 74:33-38) (Jansen, 1980:48).
2. **Muhammad Kamil Daww**: Daww argued that the scientific content in the Qur'an surpasses even its linguistic eloquence as a miracle. According to him, this reinforces both Muhammad's authenticity as a prophet and the infallibility of the Qur'an.
3. **Maurice Bucaille**: The French doctor, in his book *The Bible, The Qur'an, and Science*, claimed that while the Bible contains unscientific elements, the Qur'an aligns perfectly with modern scientific discoveries. His work has gained significant attention among those seeking to reconcile religion with science.

A More Grounded Perspective

It is important to note that not all Muslims support these interpretations. Many view the relevant verses as poetic descriptions or observations of the natural world, rather than hidden scientific prophecies. Several sayings of Muhammad himself caution against overreaching interpretations:

- **Muhammad's Warning Against Misinterpretation**:

  "Refrain from speaking about me except of what you know. Whoever speaks a lie about me deliberately, let him prepare his place in Hellfire. And whoever interprets the Qur'an by his own opinion, let him prepare his place in Hellfire." (*Tirmidhi*, Tefsir 1, no. 2951)

- **The Danger of False Attribution**:

"If anyone deliberately attributes a lie to me, their abode is Hell."
(*Abu Dawud*, vol. 3, ch. 1372, book 19, no. 3643, p. 1036)
"...And whoever intentionally ascribes something to me falsely, he will surely take his place in the (Hell) Fire."
(*Bukhari*, vol. 8, book 73, no. 217, p. 139-140)

- **False Witnessing**:

A false witness is deemed as grave as ascribing partners to Allah.
(*Ibn-i-Majah*, vol. 3, book 13, no. 2372, p. 414)

Reflection on the Debate

The Qur'an itself addresses false claims and misattributions:

"Nay, We hurl the Truth against Falsehood, and it knocks out its brain, and behold, Falsehood doth perish! Ah! Woe be to you for the (false) things ye ascribe (to Us)." (*Sura 21:19*)

This verse underscores the need for integrity when interpreting religious texts. While some may see modern science in the Qur'an, others caution against reading contemporary knowledge into ancient scriptures, warning that such overreach risks distorting the original intent and meaning.

Muslim Views and Responses

Claim 1: The Qur'an Anticipates Modern Science

The Qur'an describes the sun and moon as being in orbit and rotating along their axes (Sura 21:33; 36:27-40). It even references the Big Bang theory (Sura 21:30; Sura 51:47-48). The Arabic word *falak* is interpreted as "orbit," and the word *yasbahuna* (from *sabaha*) is claimed to mean rotating on its axis. Some argue this aligns with modern astronomical discoveries, such as the sun orbiting the galaxy every 250 million years.

Response:
This interpretation relies on wishful thinking for two main reasons:

1. **Vague Language**:
   - *Falak* in Arabic means "course" or "progress" and does not exclusively mean "orbit."
   - *Yasbahuna* can mean "hastening on" or "swimming," and its direct interpretation does not necessarily imply axial rotation.
2. **What Mohammed Said**: Mohammed's own explanation contradicts these interpretations. For example:
   - **Al-Tabari**:

     "God created an ocean three farsakhs (18 kilometers) removed from heaven... The sun, the moon, and the retrograde stars [five planets] run in its deep swell. This is (meant by) God's word: 'Each swims in a sphere.' The 'sphere' is the circulation of the chariot in the deep swell of that ocean." (*Al-Tabari, vol. 1, p. 235*)

   - **Bukhari**:

     "The Prophet asked me at sunset, 'Do you know where the sun goes at the time of sunset?' I replied, 'Allah and His Apostle know better.' He said, 'It goes (i.e., travels) till it prostrates itself underneath the Throne, and takes permission to rise again.'" (*Bukhari, vol. 4, book 54, no. 441, p. 283*)

Claim 2: The Qur'an Mentions the Sun's Orbit Around the Galaxy

Response:
The sun does not have an independent orbit within the galaxy; it moves with the solar system as a whole. If the Qur'an intended to describe this, it would have mentioned that the sun, moon, earth, and planets all move together in this galactic orbit. Again, Mohammed's explanations in *Bukhari* and *Al-Tabari* describe a geocentric model, not a heliocentric or galactic understanding.

Claim 3: The Sun's Resting Place Refers to Its Position on the Other Side of the Earth

Response:
This claim is contradicted by Mohammed's own explanation, where he described the sun traveling to a specific location under Allah's throne before rising again. (*Bukhari, vol. 4, book 54, no. 441, p. 283; Al-Tabari, vol. 1, p. 235*)

Claim 4: The Sun's Resting Place Refers to Its Ultimate Destruction

Response:
A plain reading of the verses suggests a cyclical process, not an eschatological event. There is no clear indication in the Qur'an that this refers to the sun's eventual destruction.

230

Claim 5: Language of Appearance

Some argue these verses were poetic expressions describing the observed motions of celestial bodies, not intended to support or contradict modern science.

Response:
This interpretation might seem reasonable if not for the explicit literal explanations provided in *Bukhari* and *Al-Tabari*. If their interpretations were incorrect, it raises questions about the reliability of their accounts on other matters.

Conclusion

Some Muslims attempt to use these verses to assert the scientific accuracy of the Qur'an. However, a closer examination reveals:

1. The verses are vague and open to multiple interpretations.
2. The literal explanations provided by Mohammed and early Islamic scholars contradict modern scientific understanding.
3. Claims of scientific foresight require significant reinterpretation of the text and its historical context.

To claim these verses prove the scientific accuracy of the Qur'an is not intellectually honest. In fact, some of these verses directly conflict with established scientific facts unless interpreted as poetic or metaphorical. However, historical records show that Mohammed and early Islamic scholars understood them literally, supporting a geocentric worldview where the sun and moon "swim" above the earth.

Ultimately, what matters most is not proving or disproving ancient scientific claims but understanding the spiritual and moral truths revealed by God. Every scientific paradigm evolves, and what is considered accurate today may change tomorrow. True knowledge lies in God's eternal revelation, which is preserved and guides humanity toward what is necessary for faith and life.

Bibliography

Translations of the Qur'an

1. Arberry, Arthur J. *The Koran Interpreted.* Macmillian Publishing Co., Inc., 1955.
2. Dawood, N.J. *The Koran.* Penguin Books, 1956–1999.
3. Malik, Farooq-i-Azam. *English Translation of the Meaning of AL-QUR'AN: The Guidance for Mankind.* The Institute of Islamic Knowledge, 1997.
4. Pickthall, Mohammed Marmaduke. *The Meaning of the Glorious Koran.* Dar al-Islamiyya (Kuwait), no date.
5. Rodwell, J.M. *The Koran.* First Edition. Ivy Books, Published by Ballantine Books, 1993.
6. Shakir, M.H. *The Qur'an.* Tahrike Tarsile Qur'an, Inc., 12th U.S. Edition, 2001.
7. Sher Ali, Maulawi. *The Holy Qur'an.* Islam International Publications Limited (Ahmadiyya), 1997.
8. Yusuf 'Ali, Abdullah. *The Holy Qur-an: English Translation of the Meanings and Commentary.* Revised & Edited by The Presidency of Islamic Researches, IFTA. King Fahd Holy Qur'an Printing Complex, Al Madina, Saudi Arabia, 1410 A.H.

Other References

- Campbell, Dr. William. *The Qur'an and the Bible in the Light of History and Science* (2nd edition). Arab World Ministries, 2002.
- Dr. Muhammad Muhsin Khan. *The Translation of the Meanings of Sahih Al-Bukhari Arabic-English Vol.1.* Islamic University, Al-Medina Al-Munawwara, AL MAKTABAT AL SALAFIAT AL MADINATO AL MONAWART, no date, no copyright.

- Ehsan Yar-Shater (General Editor). *The History of al-Tabari: An Annotated Translation.* State University of New York Press, 1989–.
- Debate.org. "Interpretations of the Qur'an." Accessed online.

Appendix: Translations of Sura 36:38–40

Here are various translations of **Sura 36:38–40**, showcasing how different translators interpret the verses:

M.H. Shakir's Translation *"And the sun runs on to a term appointed for it; that is the ordinance of the Mighty, the Knowing. (39) And (as for) the moon, We have ordained for it stages till it becomes again as an old dry palm branch. (40) Neither is it allowable to the sun that it should overtake the moon, nor can the night outstrip the day; and all float on in a sphere."*

M.M. Pickthall's Translation *(Verse numbering one lower than others.)*
"(37) And the sun runneth on unto a resting-place for him. That is the measuring of the Mighty, the Wise. (38) And for the moon We have appointed mansions till she return like an old shriveled palm-leaf. (39) It is not for the sun to overtake the moon, nor doth the night outstrip the day. They float each in an orbit."

Maulawi Sher Ali's Translation (Ahmadiyya) *(38)* *"And a Sign for them is the night from which We strip off the day, and lo! They are in darkness. (39) And the sun is moving on the course prescribed for it. That is the decree of the Almighty, the All-Knowing God."*

Muhammad Farooq-i-Azam Malik's Translation *(36:37–40)*
"Another sign for them is the night; when We withdraw the daylight from it, and behold they are in darkness. The sun runs its course, this course is pre-estimated for it by the Almighty, the All-Knowing. As for the moon, We have designed phases for it till it again becomes like an old dry palm branch. Neither it is possible for the sun to overtake the moon, nor for the night to outstrip the day; each floats along in its own orbit."

Yusuf Ali's Translation (Revised Edition) *(37) "And a Sign for them is the Night: We withdraw therefrom the Day, and behold they are plunged into darkness; (38) And the Sun runs its course for a period determined for it: that is the decree of (Him), the Exalted in Might, the All-Knowing. (39) And the Moon - We have measured for her mansions13 (to traverse) till she returns like the old (and withered) lower part of date-stalk. (40) It is not permitted to the Sun to catch up the Moon, nor can the Night outstrip the Day: each (just) swims along in (its own) orbit17 (according to Law)."*

Footnote 17 explains: "Circuit, course."

A.J. Arberry's Translation *"And a sign for them is the night; We strip it of the day and lo, they are in darkness. And the sun - it runs to a fixed resting-place; that is the ordaining of the All-Mighty, the All-Knowing. And the moon - We have determined it by stations, till it returns like an aged palm-branch. It behooves not the sun to overtake the moon, neither does the night outstrip the day, each swimming in a sky."*

J.M. Rodwell's Translation *"A sign to them also is the night. We withdraw the day from it, and lo! They are plunged in darkness; And the sun hasteneth to her place of rest. This, the ordinance of the*

Mighty, the Knowing! And as for the moon, We have decreed stations for it, till it change like an old and crooked palm branch. To the sun it is not given to overtake the moon, nor doth the night outstrip the day; but each in its own sphere doth journey on."

N.J. Dawood's Translation *"The night is another sign for men. From the night We lift the day - and they are plunged in darkness. The sun hastens to its resting-place; its course is laid for it by the Mighty One, the All-Knowing. We have ordained phases for the moon, which daily wanes and in the end appears like a bent old twig. The sun is not allowed to overtake the moon, nor does the night outpace the day. Each in its own orbit swims."*

Submission.org's Interpretation *"The sun sets into a specific location, according to the design of the Almighty, the Omniscient."*

Sources:

- Christian Debater™ P.O. Box 144441 Austin, TX 78714
- Various Qur'an translations and publishers, including **Pickthall**, **Yusuf Ali**, **Arberry**, **Dawood**, **Malik**, **Shakir**, and **Rodwell**.

CHAPTER 15

The Quran and the Oily Red Rose Nebula

Many Muslim websites propagate the idea of a "scientific miracle" in the Qur'an, supposedly proven by an image from NASA's Hubble Space Telescope. This image, taken on September 18, 1994, and referred to as **NGC 6543** (the Cat's Eye Nebula), gained attention within the Muslim community when it was featured on NASA's website on October 31, 1999. Since then, the claim that the Qur'an predicted this celestial phenomenon has circulated widely.

For example:

- One site states, *"They should have called it the 'Oily Red Rose Nebula.' As the Qur'an states in Surat ar-Rahman (chapter 55): 'When the sky is torn apart, so it was (like) a red rose, like ointment.' How would the Qur'an know 1,400 years ago that when a star explodes, it looks like an oily red rose?"* (Source: wideopenwest.com/~salamradio/Nebula.htm)

236

- Another claims, *"We see it now in 1999/2000, and the Qur'an mentioned it almost 1,400 years ago!"* (Source: dr-umar-azam.com)
- A similar assertion reads, *"It is amazing how accurately the Qur'an describes these events some 1,400 years ago!"* (Source: ehalal.net/Islam/iarticles/Rose%20Nebula.htm)
- Yet another asks, *"Why didn't NASA call this the 'Rose Nebula' instead of the Cat's Eye Nebula?"* (Source: Submission.org).

These claims are based on **Surah 55:37**, which states:

"When the sky is torn apart, so it was (like) a red rose, like ointment."

Key Issues with This Claim

1. Translation Variability

The primary issue lies in the Arabic word used in this verse, which is so obscure that its exact meaning is debated. Let's compare translations of Surah 55:37 to highlight the variability:

- **Pickthall:** "And when the heaven splitteth asunder and becometh rosy like red hide."
- **Yusuf Ali:** "When the sky is rent asunder, and it becomes red like ointment."
- **Shakir:** "And when the heaven splits up and turns crimson like red hide."
- **Hilali and Khan:** "Then when the heaven is rent asunder, and it becomes rosy or red like red oil, or red hide."
- **Rodwell:** "And when the heaven shall be cleft asunder, and become rose red, like stained leather."
- **Khalifa:** "When the sky disintegrates, and turns rose-colored like paint."

While most translations describe the sky becoming red, the form of a "rose" is not explicitly mentioned. Instead, comparisons are made to *ointment, stained leather,* or *red oil.* Only a minority of translators imply a resemblance to a rose. This ambiguity undermines the claim of a precise prediction of the Cat's Eye Nebula's appearance.

2. The Context of the Verse

The verse is part of a passage that describes apocalyptic events, including the heavens splitting apart. It is not a detailed scientific description of celestial phenomena. Instead, it uses vivid, poetic imagery to convey the grandeur and terror of the end times.

3. Scientific Connection

The Cat's Eye Nebula, scientifically referred to as NGC 6543, is the remnant of a dying star approximately 3,000 light-years away in the Draco constellation. It was discovered through modern telescopes, which use advanced imaging technology. Associating the Qur'anic verse with this nebula requires a leap in interpretation, as there is no direct mention of stars, nebulae, or their specific visual characteristics in the text.

4. Obscure Language as "Proof"

When the meaning of a verse is unclear, as is the case with the Arabic term in this verse, it becomes difficult to attribute a definitive, scientifically accurate interpretation. Using such ambiguity as evidence of a "scientific miracle" raises questions about whether the connection is genuinely there or imposed by modern interpreters.

Conclusion

While it is admirable to seek connections between religious texts and modern discoveries, the claim that **Surah 55:37** foretells the Cat's Eye Nebula is problematic. The translation of the verse is inconsistent, the context is apocalyptic rather than scientific, and the specific imagery of a "rose-shaped nebula" is not explicitly present in the Qur'anic text.

At best, the verse uses poetic imagery to describe the sky's transformation, which could be interpreted in many ways. The connection to the Cat's Eye Nebula is speculative and does not constitute clear evidence of scientific foreknowledge in the Qur'an.

The translations used in the various Muslim articles cited earlier remain anonymous. Some render **Surah 55:37** as follows:

- "And if the sky is torn apart to become a rose as in a painting."
- "When the sky splits apart, and turns rose-like..."
- "When the sky is torn apart, so it was (like) a red rose, like ointment."

These translations appear to have been tailored to align with the image of the nebula, but what justification exists for this? Would it not demonstrate intellectual integrity to acknowledge that the exact meaning of the word in question remains uncertain? Furthermore, these translations are inconsistent, particularly in tense: *"When the sky is (present tense)... so it was (past tense)..."* This inconsistency violates the fundamental principle of cause and effect, as a present or future event cannot logically result in a past outcome.

Misapplication of the Verse

It is crucial to note that the verse explicitly states, *"when the sky is torn apart,"* not *"when a star loses part of its substance."* The nebula's appearance, which results from a star shedding its outer layers, is only observable through advanced telescopes due to its faintness and minuscule size in the vast expanse of the sky. This raises the question:

1. **Why associate this verse with the image of the nebula?** The sky has not been "torn apart," nor has the star itself been obliterated, as evidenced by its intact core visible at the center of the image.

2. **If the verse does not describe this event, where is the miracle?**

Misinterpretation of "Sky"

One Muslim author acknowledges the problem of extrapolating a single star's image to the entire sky and suggests the verse might instead reference the Big Bang. They reason:

"The above photograph of the exploding nebula raises a distinct possibility that the explosion at some very early stage of the Big Bang might have looked like the photograph of the nebula. In that case, the Qur'anic verse in Sura Ar-Rahman is yet another reference to the Big Bang. Notice that the verse in Sura Ar-Rahman says 'when the sky is cloven apart...' and not when 'a star is torn apart...' The reference to the sky rather than a star suggests an explosion involving the whole universe as in the Big Bang."

However, this reasoning is flawed for several reasons:

1. **Context of the Verse** The Qur'anic verse refers to a **future event**, likely associated with Judgment Day or the end of the world, as supported by the context and related discussions (see *Does the Qur'an Speak About a "Lifecycle of the Universe"?*). It is not describing the beginning of the universe.
2. **Existence of the Sky** The verse implies the sky must already exist to be torn apart. However, before the Big Bang, there was no "sky" as we understand it. Thus, the connection to the Big Bang is scientifically illogical.
3. **Temporal Discrepancy** Astrophysical theories suggest the universe is billions of years old, with billions more to go before its eventual demise. The nebula image depicts a localized event in the middle of the universe's life, not its beginning or end. How, then, can a verse about the world's end be evidence for the Big Bang, particularly when tied to an image of a single star?

Conclusion

The attempt to associate **Surah 55:37** with the Cat's Eye Nebula or the Big Bang lacks logical and scientific validity. The verse's ambiguous language, its apocalyptic context, and the temporal and conceptual gaps between the nebula image, the Big Bang, and the end of the universe render this interpretation unsubstantiated.

The original information is credited to Jochen Katz of *Answering Islam*. We extend our gratitude for their meticulous work in examining these claims.

www.ingramcontent.com/pod-product-compliance
Lightning Source LLC
Chambersburg PA
CBHW061241120726
48001CB00001B/87